BLICKLING HALL

Norfolk

THE NATIONAL TRUST

This is a shortened version of the guidebook first published in 1987. It was largely written by John Maddison, the Trust's former Historic Buildings Representative responsible for Blickling. Dr John Newman contributed the chapter on the Jacobean house. The descriptions of the textiles were written by Pamela Clabburn, and Elizabeth Griffiths read and corrected the original text. Many of the Trust's staff have given their advice and expertise, and I am also grateful to the staff of the Norfolk and Norwich Record Office, and to Peter Wade of the Norfolk Archaeological Unit.

In most of the showrooms blinds are used to protect the ancient textiles and paintings from the damaging effects of light. It is hoped that visitors will understand that this protection is essential if future generations are to be able to enjoy the rooms and their contents.

Oliver Garnett

First published in Great Britain in 1987 by
National Trust (Enterprises) Ltd
© 1987 The National Trust
Registered charity no. 205846

ISBN 978 1 84359 030 9

Reprinted 1992, 1997; revised 1989, 1993, 1995
New edition 1998
Reprinted 2002, 2004, 2005, 2008, 2009, 2010; revised 2000, 2003, 2004, 2006, 2007

Photographs: British Architectural Library/RIBA, London p. 55; James Dodds p. 36; National Gallery of Scotland pp. 52, 53; National Trust pp. 4 (centre left and centre right), 31, 32, 34 (bottom left and right), 42, 48 (top and centre right); National Trust Photographic Library pp. 23, 49; NTPL/John Bethell p. 50; NTPL/Derek Croucher front cover; NTPL/John Hammond pp. 4 (far left and far right), 14, 18, 35, 44, 46, 47, 51, 54, 56, back cover; NTPL/Roger Hickman p. 5; NTPL/Horst Kolo p. 40; NTPL/Nadia MacKenzie pp. 1, 8, 9, 11, 12, 13, 15, 16, 17, 19, 21, 24, 25, 27, 29, 34 (top right), 41; NTPL/Nick Meers pp. 6, 33, 37; NTPL/Mike Williams pp. 7, 38, 39; Norfolk Museums Service p. 45.

Designed and typeset by James Shurmer

Printed by Hawthornes for National Trust (Enterprises) Ltd, Heelis, Kemble Drive, Swindon, Wilts SN2 2NA on Cocoon Silk made from 100% recycled paper

(*Front cover*) The east front

(*Title-page*) The coat of arms of the 2nd Earl of Buckinghamshire and his wife Caroline Conolly from the headboard of the bed in the Chinese Bedroom

(*Back cover*) Detail of J.H. Pollen's painted frieze in the Long Gallery

CONTENTS

BLICKLING HALL

Nobody forgets their first sight of Blickling. As the road turns past the church, the south front suddenly comes into view: a sumptuous confection of local red brick and Ketton limestone, Dutch gables and turrets, framed by massive yew hedges and service wings with even more picturesque gables. Blickling is everyone's idea of a great Jacobean country house.

Blickling Hall was built by SIR HENRY HOBART (pronounced 'Hubbard') at the end of a lucrative career as a London lawyer. When he bought the estate in 1616, it was already famous as the supposed birthplace of Henry VIII's second queen, Anne Boleyn, and Sir Henry retained much of the Boleyns' Tudor house in his new mansion, which began rising in 1619. Hobart's architect was Robert Lyminge, who had already built the even grander Hatfield House for James I's first minister, Robert Cecil. Inside, the best surviving features of Sir Henry's house are the superb plasterwork ceilings, particularly those in the South Drawing Room and Long Gallery, which were probably both executed by the plasterer Edward Stanyon.

Sir Henry died in 1625 before his new home was complete, and within 20 years decline had set in. Indeed, his great-grandson, Sir Henry Hobart, 4th Bt, almost bankrupted the estate by his obsessive political campaigns; it was saved only by his death in a duel with a political opponent in 1698.

The 4th Baronet's son, John, later 1st Earl of Buckinghamshire (1693–1756), was five years old at the time, and while he grew up, Blickling's finances recuperated. His witty and attractive sister Henrietta became the mistress of the Prince of Wales, and largely through her influence, the 1st Earl established a position at court. He celebrated his place in Norfolk's Whig hierarchy by commissioning full-length portraits of his sister (now in the South Drawing Room) and of many Norfolk grandees (over the stairs in the Great Hall). He also inherited a precious library, for which he made room in the Long Gallery.

JOHN, 2ND EARL OF BUCKINGHAMSHIRE (1723–93) was described in his youth as 'the clearcake; fat, fair, sweet and seen through in a moment'. But he grew up into a more considerable figure, who was knowledgeable about architecture both old and new. In 1762 he was appointed British Ambassador to the Court of Catherine the Great in Russia, and returned two years later with the huge tapestry of Peter the Great that now adorns the Peter the Great Room. From 1765, with the advice of his aunt

Sir Henry Hobart

The 2nd Earl of Buckinghamshire

The 8th Marquess of Lothian

The 11th Marquess of Lothian

The south front from Pond Meadow

Henrietta, he remodelled Blickling with a respect for its Jacobean origins that was unusual for the period. His architects, Thomas and William Ivory, moved the Jacobean main staircase into the Great Hall and rebuilt it as a grand double flight. They also recast the north and west fronts in a more symmetrical, but still Jacobean, form. The fashionable London architect Samuel Wyatt designed the Neo-classical Orangery and completed the State Bedroom, which was intended as a memorial to the builder of the house.

The 2nd Earl's sons died in infancy, so Blickling passed in 1793 to his daughter, Caroline, Lady Suffield, who lived quietly here for over 50 years. She called in the local architect John Adey Repton to rebuild the clock-tower that crowns the south front.

Lady Suffield's grand-nephew, WILLIAM, 8TH MARQUESS OF LOTHIAN (1832–70), inherited Blickling in 1850 at the age of eighteen. He was then a student at Oxford, where he met the decorative painter and architect John Hungerford Pollen.

Pollen painted the colourful frieze in the Long Gallery, which combines interlaced Celtic patterns with birds and animals. The 8th Marquess's wife, Constance, devoted her long widowhood to the garden, establishing the elaborate Parterre beneath the east front. After her death in 1901, Blickling was let for the next 30 years, as the Lothians had two other large houses in Scotland.

In 1932 PHILIP, 11TH MARQUESS OF LOTHIAN (1882–1940) decided to make Blickling his principal English home, and it is entirely due to his vision that the house and estate survive today. Addressing the National Trust's AGM in 1934, he set out the basis of what was to become the Country Houses Scheme, whereby, in place of death duties, whole houses and their contents could be left to the nation intact with their estate income as an endowment. The bill enacted by Parliament in 1937 has been the means by which all the Trust's major houses have been saved, beginning with his bequest of Blickling in December 1940. Blickling was thus the prototype for one of the most important conservation initiatives of our times.

TOUR OF THE HOUSE

The Exterior

The Jacobean house is built on the site of a late medieval predecessor, which determined the proportions and general arrangement of its plan (p. 34). Between 1619 and 1626 Sir Henry Hobart rebuilt the south and east fronts. The projecting wings, begun in 1624, also incorporated parts of earlier structures. It was not until the late 18th-century remodelling by the 2nd Earl that all visible trace of the earlier house was removed with the rebuilding of the north and west fronts.

THE SOUTH FRONT

Completed, according to the date stone on the parapet, in 1620. The bulls standing on the bridge are the Hobart crest; on the arch two more bulls flank the achievements of Sir Henry Hobart and his wife, Dorothy Bell. The initials H D (for Sir Henry and Dorothy) and I P for their successors, John and Philippa, decorate lead rainwater heads. On the second-floor balcony Sir Henry's legal status is reflected in the statues of Justice, with a sword and scales, and Prudence, with a mirror. On the central gable is a boy with a spear and shield, flanked, on the side gables, by Atlas figures.

The clock-tower, built by John Adey Repton after 1828, replaced an 18th-century structure. The clock is by Page and Christian of Norwich, *c*.1780. Repton was also responsible for the colonnades which link the front to its wings.

THE EAST FRONT

The east front is Jacobean throughout its length. On the first floor the windows of the Great Chamber (now South Drawing Room) and Long Gallery overlooked the garden, and at ground level were two impressive entrances. One survives beneath the southern colonnade, but the position of the other, which opened into the old stair hall, is marked by a solitary rosette in the frieze above the ground-floor windows. The doorway was removed to the north turret in the early 18th century. The statues on the gables are similar to those on the south front, and the plinth of the central one is inscribed 'DONA DEI' ('gift of God'). It may represent Charity.

The east front

THE NORTH FRONT

The square central projection with the shaped gable was probably late 17th-century, but the straight gables represent Tudor work, probably built by Sir Thomas Boleyn, that survived until the 2nd Earl's rebuilding of 1767–8. The 18th-century work is unusually faithful to the Jacobean design: only the left-hand gable and turret are actually Jacobean. The right-hand turret is partly a Tudor survival and is smaller in girth than the other three. Its windows were inserted by the 2nd Earl in 1773.

THE WEST FRONT

The Tudor front was remodelled and refaced to a design by William Ivory dated 1765. The bequest of Lady Buckinghamshire's jewels towards the cost of the project is recorded in the central inscription. It was more or less complete in 1771.

From 1864 William Burn rebuilt the front, incorporating gables and other ornaments suggested by John Adey Repton in 1821.

THE WEST WING

The stone bearing the date 1624 is set in a rebuilt gable. Only the much repaired front wall survives from this period. The brickwork is laid in the header bond as distinct from either the Jacobean house (English bond) or the east wing (Flemish bond). The blue brick diapering at the northern end suggests either a change of plan or the existence of an earlier building. The whole of the back was rebuilt by William Burn in 1864 to provide improved kitchens, sculleries, a brewery and a laundry.

THE EAST WING

The building of this wing is dated by an estimate of 1623 which amounted to £967 10s. It specified a residential part to the north, all new built, and a stable, part of which incorporated an old barn.

The brickwork may be the earliest dated example of Flemish bond in England. The iron ties in the northern gable, forming the initial letters of Henry and Elizabeth Hobart, record its repair

The west front

in 1695. It was rebuilt in 1853, but retains some of its original internal fittings, despite a serious fire in 1874.

The ground floor is now used for a restaurant, information room and shop, and the first floor is currently being used as a contemporary art gallery. The 17th-century oak staircase in the central hall came from Drury House, Great Yarmouth, and was installed in 1970.

THE ENTRANCE PASSAGE AND STONE COURT

The great timber door is much restored, but incorporates ancient work. The Entrance Passage ceiling has Jacobean plasterwork.

The Stone Court was so called in the late 17th century to distinguish it from the rear courtyard, which was then grassed. The inner arch and the

(Above) The Great Hall

date '1619' boldly set in a strapwork panel beneath the Withdrawing Chamber window were both afterthoughts. So was the decoration and enlargement of the front door of the house, now occupying the centre of the north wall, but originally specified as 'the porch dore' and set into the left hand of the two turrets. These originally projected into the space of the court but were engulfed by the enlargement of the hall by Lord Buckinghamshire in 1767, when its front wall was realigned further forward. The door was placed centrally in 1695, when the subsidence of the left-hand turret, still noticeable, necessitated repair.

Initials carved in stone or cut in lead identify the work of different periods: HD and IP in the Jacobean sections; Bs for Buckinghamshire in the frieze and lead down-pipes of the rebuilt north wall with its 18th-century Hobart bull; CL for Constance Lothian on the corner drainpipes.

The Interior

All the contents described are original to the house except where otherwise stated and whenever possible are described CLOCKWISE FROM THE ENTRANCE DOOR under their separate headings.

THE GREAT HALL

The principal room of the Jacobean house, built on the site of the medieval great hall, whose east gable is still concealed behind the right-hand wall. (The screens passage lay to the left and the dais to the right.) It became the stair hall in 1767, when the 1620s staircase was dismantled and reassembled here. The 18th-century reliefs of Elizabeth I and Anne Boleyn were inspired by figures of the Nine Worthies which had stood in the Jacobean hall.

CEILING

A deliberately archaic design of 1767 with the Hobart bull in the centrepiece.

STAIRCASE

Nearly all the Jacobean timbers were embodied in the 18th-century reconstruction. As this was to be painted, the new elements were executed in pine. The newel figures on the left-hand flight, clock-

One of the pine figures added to the staircase when it was rebuilt as a double flight in 1767

wise from the top, are: tall figure with staff, 1620s; soldier with musket and powder flasks, repaired *c.*1650; gentleman in hose, possibly 1620s; at stair foot, bearded soldier in slashed breeches with two-handed sword, 1620s. The other figures, found on the right-hand flight and gallery, are of 1767. They include a soldier in a tricorn, a kilted Highlander and a Cossack. The decoration of the left-hand newel at the stair foot dates from the 1620s and includes images of night and musical instruments of the period. Its opposite number is decorated with 18th-century instruments.

DECORATION

The present scheme of 1979–80 reproduces the Victorian decoration. In the early 19th century the staircase and reliefs were white and the walls pink.

STAINED GLASS

The window above the staircase contains panels of 15th- and 16th-century German and Flemish glass. The upper eight panels are from the monastery of Steinfeld in the Eifel region of Germany. Buckler's watercolour of the Great Hall (p. 49) suggests that they had been inserted by 1820. The glass was removed in 1935 and languished in packing cases until it was repaired and given on permanent loan to the parish church of St Mary, Erpingham, where it was installed in the east chancel window. For conservation reasons, the glass returned to Blickling in 1995, and a replica, made by Barley Studio, was installed at Erpingham. The work was funded by a donation from the Levy Bequest.

PICTURES

(A full list of all the pictures on show is available separately.)

OVER STAIRS:

The twelve full-length portraits of leading Norfolk figures come from a series mostly commissioned from William Aikman in 1729–32 by Lord Hobart, later 1st Earl of Buckinghamshire.

FURNITURE

A series of 17th-century oak elbow chairs.

Large mahogany side-table in the style of William Kent, *c.*1730.

Oriental lacquered chest on English giltwood stand, early 18th-century.

Console table with an eagle support, 19th-century.

Richly carved 17th-century Flemish oak cupboard.

Mid-17th-century oak court cupboard with an illusionistic block frieze inlaid in boxwood.

Late 18th-century sedan chair, in which Mary Anne, first wife of the 2nd Earl of Buckinghamshire, is said to have died while crossing Green Park in 1769.

Large mahogany side-table, style of Kent, *en suite* with its opposite number but with additional legs to support a marble slab, *c.*1730.

Wheel-chair that belonged to the 8th Marquess of Lothian.

CLOCKS

Bracket clock, *c.*1740, by Jeremiah Taylor of London, converted in the 19th century to 8-bell quarter-striking.

Mahogany longcase clock with an 8-day striking movement by Benjamin Lockwood of Swaffham, late 18th-century.

METALWORK

Two mid-18th-century wrought-iron locksmith's signs, Austrian or south German.

THE LOBBY

The end of a truncated passage built in 1857–8.

FURNITURE

Small settle of 1685.

CERAMICS

Large Kangxi Chinese vase, 18th-century.

THE BROWN DRAWING ROOM

Originally the chapel of the Jacobean house, consecrated in 1629. The richly ornamented mouldings of the window bays and skirting may be connected with Matthew Brettingham's work for the 1st Earl, 1745–55. In the 1760s it was given over to Lady Buckinghamshire's dressing-room and bed-chamber. Opened up into a morning-room in 1857, renamed in 1930s.

FIREPLACE

The carved spandrels with angels, *c.*1400, are thought to have come from Sir John Fastolfe's Caister Castle via the Oxnead sale of 1732. The trophied side-pieces and the inner surround date from the early 1770s, when the ensemble formed part of the organ room on the north front. It was moved here in 1858. The Fastolfe motto crowns the composition with the Buckinghamshire arms beneath.

Iron fireback, decorated with Moses and the brazen serpent, late 17th-century.

DECORATION

Redecorated in 1969, keeping the theme of Lord Lothian's colour scheme of the 1930s, but using Japanese silk wallpaper. The elaborate painted beam ceiling by J.H. Pollen (p. 53) was restored in 2007 having been hidden from view since the 1930s. Lord Lothian's curtains (machine embroidery on canvas imitating hand-worked satin stitch) remains.

PICTURES

OVER FIREPLACE:

GODDARD DUNNING (1614–after 1678)
The Artist with Still-life
Painted in 1678, when this probably amateur artist was 64.

CENTRE OF FAR WALL:

JOHN LESLIE (1822–1916)
Constance, Lady Lothian (1836–1901)
Exh. Royal Academy 1866. Lady Lothian was responsible for creating the Parterre and terraces in the east garden, visible from this room.

FURNITURE

Giltwood console table, *c.*1725, in the style of Kent with a later fossil marble top.

Small pier-glass in a shaped frame, English, early 18th-century.

Large gilt console table with veined marble top supplied by William Freeman of Norwich, early 19th-century.

Set of mid-18th-century armchairs with cabriole legs and two matching stools with original upholstery in Genoa velvet with woollen fringes.

Two lounging chairs with cane sides, part of a set of dining furniture acquired in the early 19th century.

The Brown Drawing Room before restoration of the ceiling

THE LOWER ANTE-ROOM

Originally the lower part of the Jacobean stairwell, this room became the drinking-room in 1767 and was hung with full-length portraits. In the 19th century it was a small library and in the 1930s a sitting-room. It was redecorated in the 1960s.

TAPESTRIES

Three Brussels tapestries, c.1700, with rustic scenes after David Teniers; they were probably woven in the workshops of Jodocus de Vos. Reputed to have been given to Sir Robert Walpole by Cardinal Fleury, they were purchased in 1859 from a sale at Wolterton Hall.

FURNITURE

Two rococo looking-glasses, mid-18th-century.

Satinwood and harewood writing-table with tambour front, c.1790.

Armchair with elaborately carved back in style of Giles Grendey, mid-18th-century. Cover designed by A. Wellbourne and made by A. Snowdon, 1980.

Large lacquered chest, oriental, mid-18th-century.

Two small semicircular commodes, continental, late 18th-century.

Six high-back chairs in the style of Daniel Marot. Bought by Lord Lothian in 1939 from the collection of the Countess of Carnarvon.

THE DINING ROOM

The parlour of the Jacobean house, a room used by the family for informal dining and gaming. In 1765 it was altered and refurnished by the 2nd Earl who was concerned to retain and enhance its ancient character.

CEILING AND FRIEZE

The ceiling was to have been painted with the lives of Cupid and Psyche, which may explain why it is divided into plain fields by the 18th-century moulded beams.

The Dining Room

PANELLING

The panelling and doorcases in oak and chestnut are a remarkably effective 18th-century pastiche of Jacobean work.

DECORATION

The room was painted in the 18th century and was probably white. The present dark stain is mid-19th-century.

FIREPLACE

The large oak overmantel dated 1627 bears the arms of Sir Henry Hobart and his wife Dorothy Bell. The marble fire surround is the 2nd Earl's; its tapered half-pilasters match the timber ones to either side. The white marble was no doubt chosen to match a contemporary off-white colour scheme for the woodwork. Lord Buckinghamshire was at pains to preserve the ancient chimneypiece; it was restored in his time (eg the upper frieze) and possibly again in the 1830s. The register stove of the 1760s has an iron surround and steel grate with fender, fire-irons and trivet of the same date.

PICTURE

OVER SERVING TABLE:

JAMES GUNN (1893–1964)
Philip Kerr, 11th Marquess of Lothian (1882–1940)
A posthumous portrait of the donor of Blickling.

FURNITURE

D-shaped side-table, late 18th-century.

Rosewood circular pedestal table, c.1830.

Ten-fold screen in painted and gilt leather with floral decoration on the reverse, English, 18th-century.

Two side-tables with fret decoration, c.1765.

Two brass-bound mahogany wine-coolers, c.1760.

Small fire-screen of the type known as a 'slip screen', early 19th-century.

The dining-table, c.1765, is the 2nd Earl's; some of his chairs are ranged round the table in the window bay. The high-backed William and Mary dining-chairs are from two different sets acquired by Lord Lothian in 1939.

CLOCK

Longcase clock in a burr walnut case with floral marquetry, by Nathanial Hodges of London, c.1690.

TEXTILES

Axminster carpet of Persian pattern, late 19th-century.

CERAMICS

Three Quianlong chargers, Chinese, c.1760.

Set of cut and engraved bowls and glasses, Bohemian, 19th-century.

Dinner service, Crown Derby, 19th-century.

The Kitchen

Victorian servants' hall. In those days a subterranean corridor to the left ran from here to the main kitchen in the west wing. These rooms were rearranged by Lord Lothian in the 1930s, but in Burn's remodelling, the area between here and the garden entrance was occupied by the servants' hall and butler's pantry.

THE SERVING ROOM

The bolection panelling and fireplace date from the late 17th century, when this room was made into a small parlour. By 1793 it had become 'The Confectioner's Room' and was hung with full-length portraits. It became the Serving Room in William Burn's alterations of 1864–5, when the staircase and tunnel were introduced and the sink, dresser and hot cabinet installed.

DECORATION

The present scheme, carried out in 1987, reproduces the Victorian decoration.

The tunnel leads under the entrance passage and directly into the area formerly occupied by the

THE KITCHEN

Lord Lothian moved the Kitchen into this part of the house in the 1930s.

FURNITURE

The great table, put together in the 18th century, incorporates three pillar supports, two of which originally formed corner legs of a Jacobean table, possibly the one made for the Great Chamber by Robert Lyminge in 1627 (p.41). The range by Smith & Wellstood of London was given to Blickling in 1988.

The Dutch late 17th-century carved bench at the foot of the Brown Staircase

THE BROWN STAIRCASE

Built in 1767, when the grand staircase was installed in the Great Hall. In 1865 Burn carried it down to basement level with stone flights to provide a more effective communication with the private entrance from the west garden.

FURNITURE

Dutch carved wooden seat, late 17th-century; similar to the benches in the entrance hall at Dunham Massey, Cheshire.

PICTURE

AT TOP OF STAIRS:

FRANCIS HAYMAN (1708–76)
Four Antique Sacrifices and *Mercury delivering a Message to Jupiter and Juno*
These grisailles, which formed part of the 1st Earl's decoration in the Long Gallery (p. 23), are derived from engravings of reliefs in the Arch of Constantine and in the Museo Angelonio in Rome.

THE LOTHIAN ROW

This wing, which retains survivals of the old Tudor west range, was fitted out by Lord Buckinghamshire in 1773. The bedrooms on the top floor were each known by a letter of his title, a precedent followed by the Lothians when they refurnished the bedrooms on the first floor. In 1858 Duppa & Collins of London provided wallpapers and matching chintzes. A lily of the valley pattern was used for the curtains, carpets and papers of most of the rooms, but 'T', as shown in an early 20th-century photograph, was done out in holly. The furniture, large 'white enamel' pieces lined in bird's-eye maple with chintz panels, was supplied by G.E. Burrell of Aylsham in 1861. The bedrooms were redecorated in the 1930s by the 11th Marquess in plain colours: 'L' and 'O' in blue, 'T' in peach, 'H', 'I', 'A' and 'N' in green. All have since been redecorated and refurnished.

THE CORRIDOR

PICTURES

Nine drawings by Christoph Heinrich Kniep (1755–1825), Goethe's travelling companion on a visit to southern Italy and Sicily in 1787.

TAPESTRIES

Two Brussels verdure tapestries, early 18th-century.

CLOCK

Eight-day striking longcase clock by John Scott of Edinburgh, c.1810.

THE STAIRCASE GALLERY

(See p. 23)

THE 'O' ROOM

In 1793 this was Lady Belmore's dressing-room, originally the centre of a suite of three rooms (p. 52). The white and Siena marble fireplace, c.1773, is by John Ivory, and has a contemporary Carron grate.

*The 'O'
Room*

DECORATION

The wallpaper, a copy of an early 20th-century French paper, was hung in 1974.

FURNITURE

Victorian iron and brass bedstead with an unusual mid- to late 18th-century quilted chintz counterpane (given to Blickling).

The late 18th-century mahogany pole-screen contains a piece of ancient black velvet worked with the legend 'A piece of the bed in which Anne Boleyn was born at Blickling 15 .... Beheaded 19th May 1536'. The fabric is in fact of the 1560s.

Embroidered prayer stool, mid-Victorian.

CERAMICS

Large wash-stand set by Copeland, 19th-century.

THE PRINT ROOM

A bedroom in the early 1770s, this was known as the 'Copperplate Room' in 1793. The prints found in the 'A' Room in 1974 were moved here, probably their original home, and put up with additional borders and decorative devices copied by John Sutcliffe from originals found under layers of paint in the 'A' Room. The background is the colour of the original canvas. There are 52 18th-century prints. Several are by Piranesi, including the Tomb of Cestius, which may have provided a model for the 2nd Earl's mausoleum. Others are engraved after works by Rubens, Raphael, Claude, Angelica Kauffman, Reynolds and Richard Wilson.

FIREPLACE

Marble surround by John Ivory, *c.*1773, with a more elaborate Carron grate than its counterpart in the adjacent dressing-room.

The Print Room

FURNITURE

Two painted armchairs, late 18th-century.

Rosewood pole-screen with canvas embroidered panel, late 18th-century.

Three neo-Greek chairs painted in black and gilt, early 19th-century.

TEXTILES

Modern festoon window curtains, as described in the 1793 inventory.

Carpet, Tabriz, *c*.1900.

CERAMICS

Mantelpiece ornaments, decorated with views, Barr, Flight & Barr, Worcester, *c*.1814.

THE LOTHIAN ROW
BATHROOM

Redecorated in 1972 with a reprint of an 18th-century paper border. This room originally served as a dressing-room to the West Turret Bedroom beyond and probably became a bathroom in 1858–61. The fire surround with a steel shuttered grate is mid-19th-century.

FURNITURE

Weighing chair by Youngs of London, late 19th-century.

Mahogany water closet, 1860s.

THE WEST TURRET BEDROOM

The principal bedchamber of the Jacobean house, updated *c.*1760. In 1793 it was known as the Blue Room, and traces of the dark blue paint, predating the Georgian woodwork, have been found under the wallpaper. A doorway was uncovered in the north wall, no doubt a Jacobean door communicating with the Tudor west range.

CEILING

A fine Jacobean design of straps and bosses; the cornice may have been remodelled in the 1760s.

FIREPLACE

Carved pine rococo surround of the 1760s. The Carron grate was inserted in the 1770s.

PICTURE

OVER FIREPLACE:

ANTONIO CANALETTO (1697–1768)
Chelsea from the Thames
The left half of a view painted in 1750–1; the right half is in the National Museum in Havana, Cuba.

FURNITURE

Chippendale mahogany dressing-table with lift-up top and compartments for powder, brushes, etc, *c.*1760.

Chest-of-drawers on stand with floral marquetry, Dutch, late 17th-century.

Writing-desk inlaid with floral marquetry in various woods, Dutch, late 17th-century. Both Dutch pieces much altered in the 19th century.

Brass-bound mahogany dressing-case, early 19th-century, belonging to Lord Castlereagh, Foreign Secretary, 1812–22.

TEXTILES

The modern bed and the window are hung with late 17th- or early 18th-century crewelwork. Crewelwork is a mixture of many different stitches

The West Turret Bedroom

worked on a union fabric of linen and cotton in crewel wool, a hard-wearing two-ply worsted. Two distinct sets of hangings are discernible. The side-curtains are the earlier; dating from the late 17th century, they remain in their original state. The backing fabric of the later set was replaced in 1980.

CLOCK

Eight-day spring clock in mahogany case by Alexander Leroux, London, *c.*1820.

THE WEST TURRET BATHROOM

The closet of the Jacobean bedchamber, it became a bathroom in the 1860s. The plaster ceiling is Jacobean. Pine fireplace, 1760s; Carron grate, 1770s.

PORCELAIN

Mirror (Meissen, 19th-century), shepherdesses (Vincennes) and accessories.

Ewer and basin based on a late 18th-century original by Guerhard, Paris.

THE CHINESE DRESSING ROOM

The room formed the western part of the Jacobean withdrawing chamber, divided into a bedroom and dressing-room by Lord Buckinghamshire in the early 1760s. The pine chimneypiece is of this date, the grate of the 1770s.

DECORATION

The room was originally decorated with a Chinese wallpaper, fragments of which were discovered during redecoration in 1972–3. The present paper is a modern reprint of an English paper of 1760.

(Left) Martha, Lady Drury and her daughter, Mary, the first wife of the 2nd Earl of Buckinghamshire; attributed to Thomas Hudson, 1754 (Chinese Dressing Room). Mary's jewels paid for the rebuilding of the west front

(Right) The Chinese Bedroom

PICTURE

ON EAST (FAR) WALL:

Attributed to THOMAS HUDSON (1701–79)
Martha, Lady Drury and her daughter Mary, Countess of Buckinghamshire, 1754
Mary married the 2nd Earl of Buckinghamshire in 1761 and died in 1769, bequeathing her jewels for the completion of the west front.

FURNITURE

17th-century Italian chest on late 18th-century English stand. Drawers fitted with plaques of 'ruin' marble.

Large floral marquetry cabinet, Dutch, c.1680, in the style of Van Mekeren, with evidence of considerable 19th-century alterations.

Inlaid chest on carved stand. The chest possibly north African or Hispanic, the stand English or Dutch; 19th century.

Four high-back chairs in the Dutch style with seats worked in *gros point* and flame stitch, Victorian.

THE CHINESE BEDROOM

Formed in about 1760 by partitioning the Jacobean withdrawing chamber, the room had a window overlooking the Stone Court which was blocked up in the 1760s but still retains its masonry and glazing on the exterior. While the ceiling is typically rococo, the frieze is neo-Jacobean and imitates the ornaments of the two stone Jacobean doorcases on the Staircase Gallery (p. 40).

WOODWORK

The chimneypiece, including the basket of flowers in the broken pediment, is of carved pine, *c*.1760. The grate is early 1770s. The doors and dado panelling are of the same period.

DECORATION

When Lady Beauchamp Proctor visited in 1764, she remarked that most of the apartments were hung with 'India [ie Chinese] paper', and it is clear that the wallpaper dates from the construction of the room. The piece in the overmantel is noticeably different in colour and design from the hangings of the walls.

FURNISHINGS

Bedside tables: a pair of Sheraton enclosed wash-stands, *c*.1800.

The bed is *c*.1760. Its hangings are an extremely rare survival of a Norwich shawl bedspread cut up and displayed in the 1930s by the 11th Marquess. Originally, these pieces formed a large counterpane of a type for which P.J. Knights was awarded a silver medal from the Society of Arts in 1792. These counterpanes were woven 4 yards wide without a seam. This one had a border of coats of arms (the present valance), and in the central field were the arms of Lord Buckinghamshire and Caroline Conolly (the present headboard) with Hobart bulls in the corners. The four bulls are now in the Blickling textile conservation room, the Strangers' Hall Museum, Norwich, and the Victoria and Albert Museum, London.

Mahogany corner dressing-table in the style of Gillows of Lancaster, *c*.1810.

Carved ivory pagodas, Chinese, 18th-century, believed to have come from Marble Hill (p. 47).

Unusual white japanned wardrobe with chinoiserie designs in green, similar in its decoration to the suite made by Thomas Chippendale for David Garrick's house in the Adelphi, early 1770s.

Early 18th-century lacquered chest on giltwood stand.

Oval lacquer sweetmeat box on stand, oriental, early 19th-century.

Octagonal gilt mirror, c.1790.

Finely carved chair derived from one of the patterns in Chippendale's *Director* of 1754.

CARPETS

Unusual and important Axminster carpet, late 18th-century.

Hearth rug: a Ghiordes Moslem prayer rug.

THE SOUTH DRAWING ROOM

This was the Great Chamber of Sir Henry Hobart's house. It opened directly off the Jacobean staircase, a common arrangement in great houses of this date. It was converted into a drawing-room by the 2nd Earl in about 1760. Charles II was entertained here in 1671 and it was much used by the 11th Marquess, who held meetings at the large mahogany table (p. 56).

CEILING

One of the best Jacobean ceilings in the house. Edward Stanyon's agreement dated 1620 reveals that 'for frett ceiling ... in the gallery, greate chamber, withdrawing chamber and parlor at Blickling' he was to be paid 'fyve shillings six pence a yard square measure according to such plotts and workmanship directed to me [by] Robert Lyminge his Lordship's Surveyor of the said work'. The frieze appears to have been altered in the 18th century.

CHIMNEYPIECE

The best surviving Jacobean chimneypiece at Blickling; designed and executed by Robert Lyminge, it was originally painted to resemble different marbles. The stone surround is also Jacobean. The cast-iron fireback has the arms of Elizabeth I; the burnished steel grate is late 18th-century.

PANELLING

Dado panelling, neo-Jacobean, early 1760s.

DECORATION

The room was transformed by the 11th Marquess in the 1930s. The woodwork, which had been given an oak stain by the Victorians, was stripped and the walls hung with the present painted canvas.

The South Drawing Room

PICTURE

LEFT OF FIREPLACE:

Attributed to THOMAS GIBSON (*c*.1680–1751)
Henrietta Howard, Countess of Suffolk (1681–1767)
The mistress of the Prince of Wales and the aunt of
the 2nd Earl of Buckinghamshire, whom she
advised on his remodelling of Blickling. Painted
c.1720 in masquerade dress.

FURNITURE

AROUND WALLS:

A set of eight chairs and two sofas, *c*.1780. The silk is a
1984 re-weaving of Lord Lothian's damask, itself a
revival of a 19th-century French pattern.

Two mahogany side-tables, Chippendale, *c*.1740.

Louis XV-style writing-table with gilt mounts, 19th-
century.

Louis XV kingwood commode with gilt mounts, early
18th-century.

Two lacquered cabinets on stands, oriental, late 18th-
century.

IN CENTRE OF ROOM:

A duet stool covered with a piece of Beauvais
tapestry which was part of some early 19th-century
curtains.

Low table with X-framed legs. The lacquered
top may have formed part of a late 17th-century
cabinet.

Oak gate-leg table, early 18th-century.

CLOCK

Eight-day mantel regulation in a sycamore case by
Weeks of London, *c*.1815.

CERAMICS

Two large Imari jars, early 18th-century.

A Chinese Kangxi jar with London overdecoration,
c.1820.

TEXTILES

The large sofas are covered in satin striped rayon.

Indian carpet, 19th-century. Made at the prison in
Agra where the absence of the profit motive and
rigorous inspection ensured very high standards.

THE UPPER ANTE-ROOM

Originally the upper part of the Jacobean staircase,
this space became an ante-room hung with tapestries in 1767. In the 19th century it was used as
a billiard-room. The bookcases were installed in
the 1930s, when the books were moved up from
the Lower Ante-Room.

CEILING

A fine early 17th-century design of straps radiating
from a central carved wooden boss which was
executed by Robert Lyminge himself and originally
hung over the stairwell.

DOORS AND DADOS

These were installed in 1767. Above cartouches
with the Hobart bull is a panel of heavy geometrical
ornaments simulating Jacobean work.

TAPESTRIES

The set was made at the Mortlake factory after
1657, when Philip Hollieburie petitioned the
Commonwealth Council for permission to weave
'The History of Abraham'. They are based on a
similar set woven at Brussels in 1530–40 by
Bernaert van Orley and now at Hampton Court.
The borders were probably designed by Francis
Cleyn. The subjects are: *The Parting of Abraham from
Lot at Bethel; Sara sending her Egyptian maidservant
Hagar away with the infant Ishmael; Melchizedek
offering Bread and Wine to Abraham after the Slaughter
of Chedorlaomer and the Kings that were with him; A
Soldier with a Lance; King Abimelech; Sara; King
Abimelech taking Sara from Abraham.*

The three single figures are additions by the Mortlake factory but the other scenes are drawn from the
ten large tapestries in the Brussels set. The tapestries
are the subject of a twelve-year conservation
programme by the Blickling textile workroom.

CARPET

An important Axminster carpet of the late 18th
century with Palladian guilloche border and a floral
centrepiece.

FURNITURE

Lacquered chest on stand, oriental, 18th-century.

Six high-back chairs, mid-17th-century, with
'Norwich Red' moreen cushions, *c*.1800.

Two Chinese Chippendale silver tables with fret galleries.

CERAMICS
Nodding mandarin, oriental, late 19th-century.

BRONZES
Silenus holding the Infant Bacchus and *Venus and Cupid*, ? French, *c.*1700.

CLOCK
Eight-day English skeleton clock, *c.*1860.

THE STAIRCASE GALLERY

Formed in 1767, when the front wall of the Great Hall was moved outwards into the courtyard. At the same time the two richly carved Jacobean door-cases were moved here from the old staircase.

FURNITURE
Cassone, 19th-century, incorporating three mid-15th-century Florentine panel paintings.
Two oak hall-chairs with cabriole legs, Victorian.

CERAMICS
Vase by the Martin Brothers, late 19th-century.
Pair of Quianlong Chinese fish bowls, *c.*1760, on contemporary English giltwood stands.

THE LONG GALLERY

The Jacobean Long Gallery, 123 feet in length, was used by the 1st Earl for the display of his series of full-length portraits (p. 9). The equestrian portrait of George II (now in the Peter the Great Room) may have hung on the end wall. The room became a library *c.*1745 with the inheritance of the Ellys books (p. 25), and the grisailles by Haymans (p. 14) were painted as overdoors for it. Between 1858 and 1863 its decoration was transformed once more by J.H. Pollen for the 8th Marquess of Lothian.

CEILING PLASTERWORK

Edward Stanyon carried out the intricate pattern of embossed ribs, studded with pendants delineating 31 major panels. The eleven central panels contain heraldic achievements and symbols of the Five Senses and of Learning ('Doctrina'). The latter image and the series of 20 emblems which run down either side of the ceiling were chosen from Henry Peacham's *Minerva Britanna* of 1612. Copies of the relevant plates and the accompanying texts may be examined by visitors. In certain parts of the frieze (especially over the fireplace) it is possible to detect sections of 18th-century plasterwork carefully arranged to match the old work, probably by 'Newman Plaisterer', who was paid £44 9s 3d for work in the Long Gallery shortly after 1745.

(Left) Sara *from the* History of Abraham *tapestries, woven at Mortlake after 1657 (Upper Ante-Room)*

The Long Gallery

FIREPLACE

The Siena marble fireplace for which Joseph Pickford was paid no less than £192 13s 5d in the mid-1740s was replaced in 1858–63 by J.H. Pollen's huge hooded stone chimneypiece (illustrated on p. 55), which was, in turn, removed by the 11th Marquess in the 1930s. The spectacular steel firedogs were made by Joshua Hart & Sons to the specification of Pollen, who may also have designed the cast-iron fireback. The fire-irons and the twisted bar were the work of the estate blacksmith John Salmon. The wooden bolection surround was installed in 1972.

PAINTED FRIEZE

This is entirely the work of J.H. Pollen (p. 53), though the boards on which it is painted are possibly part of the room's mid-18th-century fittings. The panel over the book cupboard door was painted by Anna Wellbourne in 1975–6, when the frieze, which had faded badly, was restored and retouched. The 11th Marquess obscured Pollen's painted decoration on the window recesses.

STAINED GLASS

The upper lights of the north window contain heraldic panes executed in 1861 by Powells of Whitefriars to designs by J.H. Pollen. From left to right the arms are Jedburgh, Ancram, Lothian, Hobart and Britiffe. The glass is surprisingly broadly handled for its date; in this, and in its deliberate use of unevenly coloured pieces, it anticipates Arts and Crafts stained glass.

BOOKCASES

Designed by Benjamin Woodward and carved by John O'Shea with naturalistic foliage, they incorporate the carcasses of the 1st Earl's bookcases. The carving is unfinished (p. 54) and preliminary cutting-out on the side of one press near the south end shows how much more was proposed.

BOOKS

Blickling possesses what is still one of the most remarkable country-house libraries in England and the finest in the care of the National Trust. None of the Hobarts' books remains at Blickling, but in 1745 the 1st Earl of Buckinghamshire inherited the library of his distant kinsman, Sir Richard Ellys, 3rd Bt (c.1674–1742), of Nocton in Lincolnshire. Ellys spent large sums at the great book sales of the 1720s and 1730s in England and on the Continent, with the advice of his librarian John Mitchell, who compiled a manuscript catalogue. He was particularly interested in philology, buying many works on Greek and Latin, as well as on oriental languages. The collection is also rich in versions and translations of, and commentaries on, the Bible, in histories and topographies of the ancient and modern worlds, and in works on the politics, laws and customs of England. Ellys had a keen eye for the rare and curious and for fine bindings. In 1932 the 11th Marquess was obliged to sell 160 lots of books in New York to pay death duties, but most of these came from Newbattle Abbey, and Ellys's library survives virtually intact at Blickling.

FLOOR

The patterned border, now much worn, is by Pollen.

TAPESTRY

Jacob and Esau, Brussels, mid-17th-century.

FURNITURE

AT SOUTH (NEAR) END:

The chair of state is recorded in the 1793 inventory for the South Drawing Room as 'The Chair of State in which King James II sat when in Ireland – given to Lord Buckinghamshire by the Earl of

Clanbrassil'. At some stage it has been deprived of its tasselled cushions, shorn of its fringes and re-covered.

Two large chests, one 17th-century and decorated with poker-work, the other an oriental lacquered chest of the early 18th century.

IN WINDOW BAYS:

Two mahogany library tables with Chinese Chippendale brackets, probably part of the 1st Earl's library furnishings.

Mahogany benches with multiple legs and contemporary 'Norwich Red' moreen tops, early 19th-century. They become library steps when set on end.

The Long Gallery firedogs were designed by J.H. Pollen in the early 1860s and feature the 'sun-in-splendour' from the Lothian coat of arms

Armchair with swept legs and cane seat, also converts into library steps, early 19th-century.

IN FRONT OF PRESSES:

Low spindle-backed chairs also upholstered in 'Norwich Red', late 18th-century.

NEAR FIREPLACE:

Four stick-backed Windsor chairs; sophisticated late 18th-century mahogany versions of their rustic prototypes.

PIANO

Forte-piano by Joseph Kirkman in rosewood case, 1829.

THE TURRET STAIRCASE

The upper part was a closet to the Long Gallery and has a fine Jacobean ceiling with the Hobart bull in the centre. The panelling is *c.*1730, and the staircase was inserted in 1773 to communicate between the Library and Lord Buckinghamshire's Study beneath.

THE PETER THE GREAT ROOM

Work on fitting out this room took place in 1778–82.

CEILING

William Wilkins of Norwich, grandfather of the architect of the National Gallery, executed the plasterwork to William Ivory's drawings. The design derives from the illusionistic ceilings discovered in Pompeii and Herculaneum in the mid-18th century, some of which had octagonal centres and rising tabernacles occupying the corners. The latter are represented in flattened and simplified form in the irregular pentagonal corner compartments. The Hobart bulls are displayed in medallions at either end with Lord Buckinghamshire's arms in the centre. The masks of the frieze imitate Jacobean ornaments.

FIREPLACE

In 1778 John Ivory was paid 100 guineas for the 'statuary sienna chimneypiece'. The grate, surround, fender and fire-irons are contemporary.

DECORATION

This room was redecorated in 1987. The ceiling is recorded in 1806 as 'having the four corner compartments with that in the middle … stained a delicate pink' and this, together with the colour of the wall-hanging, has formed the basis of the present scheme. The new silk worsted 'half damask' has been copied from surviving fragments of the 18th-century silk and woven to the original 21-inch width on the handlooms at De Vere Mills, Castle Hedingham, Essex.

PICTURES

ON EAST (NEAR) WALL:

JOHN WOOTTON (1682–1764) and CHARLES JERVAS (*c.*1675–1739)
King George II on horseback
Painted shortly before 1732. Jervas painted the King's face, Wootton the rest.

LEFT OF FIREPLACE:

THOMAS GAINSBOROUGH (1727–88)
Caroline Conolly, Countess of Buckinghamshire, 1784
The 2nd Earl's second wife.

RIGHT OF FIREPLACE:

THOMAS GAINSBOROUGH (1727–88)
John, 2nd Earl of Buckinghamshire (1723–93), 1784
Painted in his robes as Lord Lieutenant of Ireland.

FURNITURE

The furnishing of the room corresponds almost exactly to the 1793 inventory: '2 cabriole sophas; 4 Pillows; 4 Elbow Chairs; 10 small Do cover'd the same as the Room with strip'd Manchester Cases; 4 Needlework Stools and Cases as above', and is laid out formally as in the 2nd Earl's time.

The seat furniture is typical of the designs which Hepplewhite was to publish in his *Cabinet Maker* and *Upholsterer's Guide* of 1788, although surprisingly for a room of such grandeur they are executed in plain mahogany.

The three large pier-glasses with their gilt Maratta frames and heraldic crestings, the frames of the Gainsboroughs and the even larger frame of the tapestry were all supplied by Solomon Hudson of Great Titchfield Street, London, who was paid the huge sum of £406 6s 6d in 1782 for these and two more in the State Bedroom.

The Peter the Great Room

Only the marble of the two pier-tables described in 1793 survives. The frames were renewed by William Freeman & Co. of Norwich in the early 19th century.

TAPESTRY

The tapestry of *Peter the Great triumphing over the defeated Swedish army at Poltawa in 1709* was given to the 2nd Earl by Catherine the Great at the end of his Embassy in 1765. Woven at St Petersburg in 1764, it relates to a tapestry of 1722, now in the Hermitage, St Petersburg, which is based on a design by the Russian court painter Louis Caravaque. The Blickling tapestry has a more detailed background and a border of coats of arms lacking in the 1722 version.

CARPET

The Axminster, which can only have been made for this room, is a mixture of old-fashioned and up-to-date motifs. The red guilloche border resembles a Palladian ceiling of the mid-18th century, while the centrepiece, the garlands, bouquets and large rosettes are more reminiscent of the 1770s.

CHANDELIER

Sixteen-light crystal chandelier, English, c.1775–80.

ON MANTELPIECE:

Pair of crystal candelabra, by William Parker, c.1781.

CLOCK

Eight-day French striking mantel clock, c.1820, in an ormolu and red marble case. The movement is stamped 'Hemon, à Paris'.

THE STATE BEDROOM

William Ivory submitted drawings for the frieze and cornice of the 'State Dressing room' in April 1779, but it seems unlikely that these plans were acceptable to Lord Buckinghamshire, and Samuel Wyatt may have been asked to design this room in about 1780 (p.51). The placing of the state bed behind the pillars of an alcove is a deliberately archaic arrangement appropriate to a room intended as an inner sanctum, reflecting not only the prestige of the then owner but also the fact that Blickling was founded by James I's Lord Chief Justice, whose portrait was the only picture hung in the room in 1793. The carved wooden frieze of swags and ox masks refers to the Jacobean decoration of the entrance front and the Hobart crest.

FIREPLACE

The marble surround is different in character from John Ivory's fireplaces in other rooms both in its ornament and the balance of its colours – pure white marble with Siena plaques. The burnished steel register stove, fender and fire-irons are contemporary.

DECORATION

The present hangings, which are close to the colour of original fragments, date from 1981. The crimson braid is a feature of the original decoration.

PICTURE

OVER FIREPLACE:

DANIEL MYTENS (c.1590–1647)
Sir Henry Hobart, 1st Bt (d.1626)
The builder of Blickling, painted in 1624, at the end of his life. One of Mytens's finest works.

FURNITURE

The white and gilt pole-screen and octagonal table are part of the original furnishings. The latter has an interesting top: a design on paper under glass, similar to a late Roman ceiling.

The suite of white and gilt chairs and stools is described in the 1793 inventory and is similar in design to the contemporary but less ornate mahogany suite in the Peter the Great Room.

LEFT OF FIREPLACE AND OPPOSITE:

The fine serpentine commode with ormolu mounts and the similar dressing-table are probably by John Cobb who was paid £86 in 1762 by Lord Buckinghamshire for unspecified items.

The tester and headboard of the bed are made up of a canopy of state issued to Lord Buckinghamshire in 1763 for his embassy to St Petersburg and made by William Vile and John Cobb. The arms of George II appear on the headboard but those on the counterpane are Queen Anne's. Two different damasks are used.

FLANKING BED:

The two commodes are also likely to be Cobb's work.

The State Bedroom

ABOVE:

The looking-glasses have rich rococo frames, 1760s.

The pier-table is listed in the 1793 inventory. The glass above it was made, together with the frame for Sir Henry Hobart's portrait, by Solomon Hudson in 1782.

CARPET

Axminster, made for this room and one of the superlative examples of its period. Its design partly reflects the garlanded foliage of the ceiling, but the strong black border with its swags of flowers and crimson lines is related to Roman mural decoration.

The contemporary bed carpet, of three strips sewn together, is a rare survival. The only other one is at Osterley Park.

THE STAIRCASE

The staircase was built in 1967. The plaster ceiling and dado panelling of the former State Bedroom closet remain in the upper part.

THE DOCUMENT ROOM

This was the bedroom of the 11th Marquess in the 1930s and is now used for the display of documents, books, drawings and other memorabilia relating to him and to Blickling.

THE GARDEN

Since the 17th century the main garden at Blickling has been on the east side of the house. Robert Lyminge certainly had a hand in the first layout, and the annotations on his drawing for a 'banketting house' (illustrated on p. 42) betray important clues about the overall design of Sir Henry Hobart's vanished garden. The wall in which this covered seat was set faced the house, on a terrace or 'high walk' which was clearly parallel with the east front. It would have formed one side of a formal garden whose centrepiece was perhaps a white marble fountain for which Thomas Larger was handsomely paid in 1620. The 'banketting house' drawing also makes clear that the 'high walk' led north to a wilderness, which was no doubt a second rectangular enclosure containing a geometrical layout of walks and hedges. The large square of water which once lay before the north front was known in the late 17th century as the 'Wilderness Pond', presumably because it formed one side of this wilderness. Two further features may have defined the central axis of the Jacobean garden. One was a dove-house which the survey commissioned in 1729 illustrates at the garden's southern extremity, and the other may be an early mount, largely demolished in 1688–9, whose remains could be indicated by the curving brick Victorian bastion to the north of the present Parterre. This strong north/south axis explains something about the design of the Jacobean east front and its asymmetrically placed garden door; this was an elevation to be viewed diagonally and not frontally, as it is seen today.

The late 17th-century Hobarts seem to have made their own contribution to the old layout before the entire scheme was swept away, a transformation made clear by an ostentatious survey map, decorated with the recently acquired Order of the Bath, which the future 1st Earl of Buckinghamshire commissioned from James Corbridge in 1729. It shows that in the early 18th century the whole garden was turned through 180 degrees to achieve a more expansive, if less intricate, plan, in which the most powerful axis now ran from west to east, from the house to the temple.

These great new pleasure grounds probably extended north and involved the building of the new mount. They incorporated the old square Wilderness Pond, creating a new and complex woodland area, laid out on a grid of intersecting paths at the eastern boundary of the park. A huge terrace was thrown up here to complete the design and provide views to the more distant landscape, while the Doric temple which stood in the midst of this great earthwork dominated a new and imposing vista that ran down to the house.

The geometrical woodland layout in its original form did not survive long; in the 1760s it was planted up by the 2nd Earl, who created an informal network of meandering paths that reflected his alterations to the wider landscape of the park. The principal flower garden at this time was an oblong enclosure made out of the northern portion of the woodland area. It was the domain of Lady Buckinghamshire and in 1765 contained 'the greatest profusion of Minionet Roses, mirtles and honeysuckles'. Some of the 1st Earl's garden ornaments had been purchased from the sale of Oxnead in 1732 – the statue of Hercules, now in the Orangery, and the fountain placed in the centre of the Parterre – and in the same way the 2nd Earl in 1787 bought a screen of columns from the partial demolition of nearby Irmingland Hall. At various points in the garden the Buckinghamshires placed 'seats', white-painted timber shelters with tarred roofs and backs. But the most important garden building of the late 18th century was the Orangery, built in 1782 on the southern boundary of the garden and overlooking what has been known ever since as Greenhouse Park.

Lady Suffield employed Humphry Repton's son John Adey at Gunton, and at Blickling after 1823. Many of the drawings are extremely rapid sketches which, for the younger Repton, completely deaf from birth, must have been an essential means of communication with his client. Perhaps some of them are hers. They include designs for trellises, pedestals, alcove seats, a charming little temple built of rustic poles, its pediment crested and swagged with fir cones, and a design dated 1823 for a Hardenburg basket which Repton first designed for Prince Hardenburg's seat at Potsdam in 1821–2.

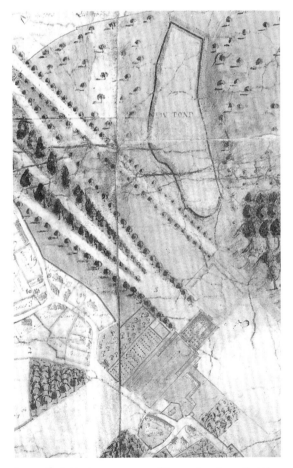

James Corbridge's 1729 survey of the garden shows that the main axis now ran from west (top left) to east (bottom right)

Several drawings are similar in their details to the trellis seat which still stands in the Secret Garden.

It is unlikely that Lady Suffield's extensive work did more than reinforce the informal framework developed by the 2nd Earl, and it was left to her successors, the Lothians, to bring the evolution of the garden full circle by resurrecting some of the 1st Earl's geometric planting designs. The first stage of this work was accomplished in 1863–4. The margin of the lake was pushed back from the house, new terraces made, old ones reshaped and enlarged, and a simplified version of the intersecting walks indicated by the Corbridge survey laid out and planted up.

This return to formality is characteristic of country-house gardening after 1840. But the revival of the 18th-century woodland design at Blickling was an unusual and most successful experiment. It necessitated the reduction of the Georgian flower garden to the small area now occupied by the Secret Garden, and in March 1870 the architect Matthew Digby Wyatt was involved in a detailed discussion with the landscape engineer Markham Nesfield over the execution of a plan for a great new flower garden on the east front. The extensive lawn which hitherto had swept up under the trees of the woodland area was now to be excavated and curtailed by a buttressed brick wall with flights of steps and bays for seats. This very considerable undertaking was completed by 1872, but in the interests of economy it had been decided that all the stone ornaments should be added later.

Neither Wyatt nor Nesfield was involved in the layout of the Parterre; this most elaborate pattern of beds, ribbon borders and hedges was entirely Lady Lothian's creation and was carried out by the head gardener, Mr Lyon. The fountain from Oxnead was placed in the centre in 1873. The correspondent of *The Garden* recalled in 1903 that the late Lady Lothian 'had such a tender heart for the gardeners who had grown old in her service that, instead of pensioning them off, she kept them about the place to do light work'. In this way a staff of fifteen gardeners was retained at Blickling until her death.

Two years before the 11th Marquess moved to Blickling in 1932, Christopher Hussey had written

The Parterre in 1920

critically of Lady Lothian's Parterre in *Country Life*: 'To the modern eye the pattern area is too small in scale. The lines of the design are lost in a multiplicity of dotted beds, beautifully filled but without a perceptible reaction to each other or to the house.' It was a natural reaction of the period and perhaps something of a consolation to the 11th Marquess, who would not have wished to keep the large garden staff necessary for its maintenance. He also had the good fortune at this juncture to meet Norah Lindsay, who is only now achieving recognition as one of the great gardeners of the 20th century. It is conceivable that Kerr met her through the Astors at Cliveden, but her first visit to Blickling was an expedition from Houghton, where she was staying with the Cholmondeleys.

Norah Lindsay spent much of her life moving from one country house to another making deft

and brilliant adjustments to their ancient gardens. At Blickling she always stayed in the Chinese Bedroom and the staff still remember the primrose scent that used to pervade that part of the house after her visits. Her reputation at this stage rested principally on Hidcote in Gloucestershire, where for several years she had been planting with Lawrence Johnston a garden of enduring beauty and fame, and upon her own garden at Sutton Courtenay, which she had published in *Country Life* in 1931. She is usually characterised as a disciple of Gertrude Jekyll and it is clear that she developed Miss Jekyll's ideas on the choice and grouping of herbaceous plants. But she was never hidebound by theory, and her approach to the remodelling of the Blickling Parterre and the Temple Walk shows how sensitive she was to their inherent qualities and potential. The yew pillars and 'grand-pianos' of the Parterre she kept, but the conifers which marched in an orderly procession to the Temple she removed, thus immeasurably improving the sense of scale. The Temple was now to be surrounded by azaleas in subtly graded colours, merging into the shade of the overhanging trees. In the Parterre the myriad of miniscule beds was replaced by four large squares banked up into the centre to provide a magnificent display of herbaceous plants in graduated colours, predominantly pink, blue, mauve and white near the house, but yellow and orange to the east. In the shelter of the Parterre's southern wall she made another long herbaceous border whose quieter colours provide a foil for the main beds.

The spring is always rather late in Norfolk and the succession of flowering at Blickling begins in late February with carpets of snowdrops beneath the cherries above the south border. In April the west garden takes over with a great display of daffodils under magnolias. The terrace is also covered with daffodils at this time and in May Mrs Lindsay's azaleas and the Victorian rhododendrons begin to add their colours to the woodland walks. The herbaceous beds flower from June to September. Several splendid *Magnolia grandiflora* on the front of the house keep their large pale flowers into the autumn, when the softly decaying colours of the native trees and the glowing tones of the red oaks in the arboretum signal the onset of winter and the period when the garden staff, now five permanent gardeners, undertake some of the major tasks of the year.

The trimming of Blickling's famous yews begins in August with the great hedges. The topiary of the Parterre is not tackled until September. The task is accomplished with mechanical cutters in little over a fortnight, but not without scaffolding and constant attention to form and line. Many of the herbaceous cultivars are now rare and in some cases unobtainable, so in the east lawn at Blickling four square beds are arranged in blocks of carefully graded colour. All are surrounded by a symmetrical planting of roses edged with catmint, with clipped yews marking the corners.

The Parterre planting today

BLICKLING AND ITS OWNERS

THE MEDIEVAL AND TUDOR HOUSE

Blickling was an old and romantic house long before its rebuilding by Sir Henry Hobart in 1619. In 1378 the southern section of the manor came into the possession of Sir Nicholas Dagworth, who settled there twelve years later after a distinguished military and diplomatic career in the service of Edward III. He built a rectangular moated house, whose plan and structure was to have a powerful influence on the layout and dimensions of the Jacobean building. Dagworth died in 1401 and is commemorated in a splendid brass in the church.

Sir Thomas Erpingham, who bought Blickling from Dagworth's widow, was a man of even greater public prominence, being appointed one of the commissioners to receive Richard II's renunciation of the throne in 1399. In 1432 Blickling was bought by Sir John Fastolfe, another famous soldier whose name, subtly altered, was borrowed for Shakespeare's comic hero in *Henry IV*. At this time one of the most powerful men in Norfolk, Fastolfe owned many houses. He died at Caister Castle in

Sir John Fastolfe's crest and arms appear in the Brown Drawing Room chimneypiece; the early 15th-century carving came originally from Caister Castle

1459, having sold Blickling to his neighbour and protégé, Geoffrey Boleyn.

Geoffrey's grandson, Sir Thomas Boleyn, was among Blickling's most important and significant owners. He made a place for himself at Henry VIII's court by capitalising on the King's ardent interest in his daughters, first Mary and then her younger sister Anne. Honours were heaped upon him in the 1520s: first Treasurer of the Household, then Knight of the Garter, Viscount Rochford and finally, in 1529, the earldom of Wiltshire. In 1533 Anne Boleyn became Queen, only to be executed with her brother three years later. She is tradition-ally said to have been born at Blickling, and this tradition was one of the most important elements of the house's pedigree as far as the Hobarts were concerned.

After Sir Thomas's death in 1539, the property passed through his brother's hands into the posses-sion of his relatives, the Cleres. Sir Edward Clere, who had dissipated his family's impressive wealth, died a bankrupt in 1605, and eleven years later his widow sold Blickling to Sir Henry Hobart.

Tomb brasses of two early owners: (left) Sir Nicholas Dagworth (d.1401); (right) Sir Thomas Boleyn (d.1539)

THE JACOBEAN HOUSE

Sir Henry Hobart came from a legal family whose most celebrated member was his great-grandfather, Sir James Hobart, Attorney-General to Henry VII. He bought the Blickling estate in 1616, but must have had his eye on it for many years. In 1590 he had been married in Blickling church, even though his bride, Dorothy Bell, came from Upwell in the far west of the county, and his family seat was south of Norwich at Intwood. His first acquisition of land in Blickling parish seems to have come years later in 1609. However, when he at last gained possession of the Hall itself, he soon set about building operations. By this time he was an elderly man – his year of birth is unknown, but was probably around 1560 – and he had long been at the summit of a distinguished and lucrative legal career. In 1611 he had been appointed Lord Chief Justice of the Common Pleas, and was among the first crop of baronets of the new order that was created in that year.

Sir Henry Hobart (d.1625), the builder of Blickling; by Daniel Mytens, 1624 (State Bedroom)

In London Sir Henry had a house in St Bartholomew's, Smithfield, rented from the Earl of Westmorland, and he also occupied a richly furnished suburban house at Highgate, the freehold of which he was still negotiating to purchase at the time of his death. In Norwich he leased Chapelfield House, which remained a residence of the Hobarts until the mid-18th century. It was natural that such a man should want to perpetuate his achievements by erecting a house that matched his status. The puzzle is that he should have waited so long. Perhaps he risked this delay because of his determination to acquire Blickling. The estate cost him £5,500, a price that was little more than half the sum he subsequently spent on rebuilding. His dynastic intentions are implied by the initials carved in stone in the spandrels of some of the doorcases of his new mansion and cast in lead on the rain-water hoppers. As well as H for himself and D for his wife, there are I for his son John and P for John's wife Philippa. Yet the dates 1619 and 1620 are just as prominent on the building – these were the years in which the walls were erected and the roofs set on – as if there was also to be a permanent reminder that it was Sir Henry's generation which had established what he hoped would become a dynasty.

It is also significant that Sir Henry decided not to abandon the moated site for one which, only slightly more elevated, could have given the expansive views beloved of so many Elizabethan and Jacobean builders. His decision to make use of part of the pre-existing fabric of Blickling Hall was not an exceptional one, but it saddled his architect with considerable problems in planning the new house.

'The architect and builder of Blickling Hall' was Robert Lyminge. That is how he is described in the Blickling parish register on his death in 1628, although elsewhere he is referred to as 'your lordship's surveyor' and 'the contriver of your lordship's works'. He received a wage of 2s 6d per day during the period of construction in recognition of his role as supervisor of the works. In choosing him Hobart had gone to one of the most experienced men of the day: from 1607 to 1612 Lyminge had been employed in a similar capacity by Robert Cecil, Earl of Salisbury, in building Hatfield House, one of the most sumptuous and expensive houses of the period. The stylistic connections between Hatfield and Blickling are obvious: the angle turrets that define the bulk of the building, the shaped gables that punctuate the skyline, the entablatures that mark the floor levels and bind all the complexities of mass together. Hatfield, however, had been built on a new site. How did Lyminge respond to the challenge of incorporating so much of the old house into his new design at Blickling?

In the west range at Blickling, where the service rooms lay, Hobart was satisfied with reroofing and internal replanning. Since the whole range was later remodelled, we can only say that there were the usual rooms: servery and kitchen, with a timber screen between them, and a bridge across the moat from the kitchen, scullery, buttery, pantry, and wet and dry larders.

The parts that Lyminge was required to form into coherent architectural compositions were the south façade, the east front towards the garden, and the front, or inner, courtyard. Certain problems confronted him: the narrowness of the entrance front, the approach to the hall and the rest of the interior of the house through an uncomfortably tight courtyard, and access to the upper floor at a point which made it impossible to arrange the principal suite as a single sequence. In solving these problems, he was led to site the main staircase in the east range so that it was approached from the hall through a lobby off the dais and thus gave room in the south-east corner of the house for a spacious parlour (now the Dining Room) on the ground floor with the great chamber (now the South Drawing Room) directly above. The withdrawing chamber which opened off the great chamber found its place in the centre of the south front above the entry passage, the principal bedchamber beyond it in the south-west angle, with a closet in the south-west angle tower. The Long Gallery could not be integrated with these three rooms and

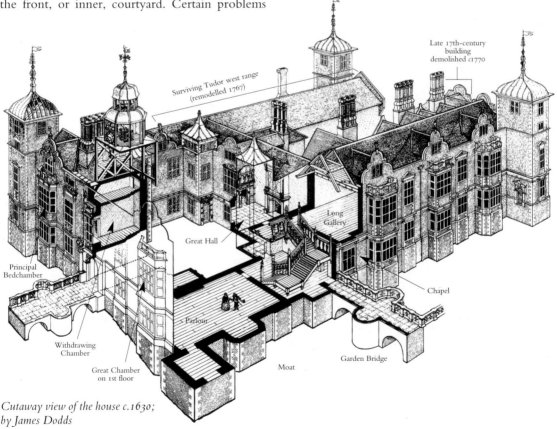

Cutaway view of the house c.1630;
by James Dodds

The south front

was placed on the other side of the great staircase. Here, in the east range, it could extend to the impressive length of 123 feet, and a second little closet was contrived in the north-east turret off its far end. The Long Gallery also gained a fine view of the gardens, which lay on the east side of the house.

The awkward feature of this arrangement was the exposed placing of the three principal chambers across the entrance front of the house so that the view from their windows was directly into the outer court. This may have been the primary cause of the exceptionally impressive treatment of the approach to the house.

Every visitor must gasp at the first sight of Blickling Hall, framed at the end of an immense formal space between two identical service ranges, each 225 feet long and embellished with gables more elaborate than those on the house itself. Elizabethan and Jacobean designers normally left such service buildings out of the composition. So it was a brilliant stroke of Lyminge's to use them to form a grand forecourt which both enhanced the dignity of the narrow-fronted house, and suitably distanced the principal chambers in the entrance range from the outside world. The service ranges, though they were presumably envisaged from the beginning, were not built until 1623–4, when the house itself was largely finished.

But how was Blickling Hall built? There are two

aspects to this: the financial and the constructional. Hobart was in the fortunate position of being able to pay for his building entirely out of rents. In each of the three years 1619–21 his steward, Richard Burton, earmarked for the purpose rents received the preceding year. During the first two years work went ahead fast and costs were commensurately high, well over £2,000 in each year, so for 1621 Hobart set a ceiling for expenditure at a much lower level. Not surprisingly, his figure of £600 was exceeded, but work did slow down sharply. In July 1625 Hobart estimated that all would be finished by midsummer the following year. However, this was a day he did not live to see. After his death in December 1625, his heir found that a number of finishing touches were required, and Lyminge himself was still being paid small sums for works in the house and garden until his death in early 1629.

At the start of building Hobart entered into a contract with a team of three master-craftsmen: Lyminge, who was a carpenter by trade, and two masons, Thomas Thorpe and Thomas Style. This was probably on 18 December 1618, when Hobart met them in London and made them an initial payment of £100. Both masons were men of considerable experience. Thomas Thorpe of Kingscliffe, brother of John Thorpe the surveyor and son of a distinguished Northamptonshire master mason, had worked for the Crown at Eltham Palace in 1603–4 and at the Banqueting

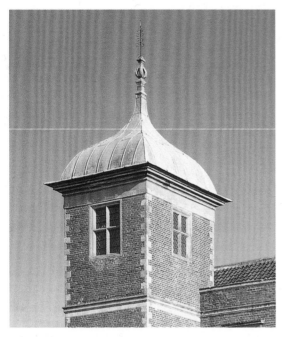

The north-west corner turret

House, Whitehall, the short-lived predecessor to Inigo Jones's building, in 1606–9. Thomas Style, who was probably a younger man, came to Blickling straight from executing the masonry contract for the King's Lodging in Newmarket in 1614–17. Lyminge, Thorpe and Style's original contract with Hobart has not survived, but they clearly undertook to carry out themselves, or with sub-contractors, the masonry, carpentry and brick-work, ie the carcass of the house. Payments to the partnership were made, sometimes weekly, on the presentation of bills. This arrangement seems to have been terminated in September 1621, when Thorpe and Style must have departed, leaving Lyminge resident at Blickling in sole charge of all the works.

The building costs can be assessed reasonably accurately from the accounts. The total for the house itself was just under £8,000, while the two service wings were rather more than £960 apiece. By the time Sir John Hobart, Sir Henry's son, had laid out further sums on final items of carpentry, joinery and furnishings, Blickling Hall must have cost the family over a decade something in excess of

£10,000. In comparison, the recorded expenditure on the building of Hatfield House between 1607 and 1612 amounted to £38,848, but it was among the grandest country houses of the period. Trentham Hall, a gentry house in Staffordshire, cost £6,165 17s 4d to erect between 1630 and 1638.

Building materials were as local as possible. Bricks were made on the estate in three specially constructed kilns, 823,000 in 1619 at 5s per thousand, 465,500 in 1620 at the lower price of 4s 6d per thousand, and in 1621–2, when the carcass of the house was largely complete, 125,000 more. Two years later the service ranges probably required a further million. The brick kilns may have been up to a mile away, for carriage of bricks was not cheap at 1s per load. Lime could also be produced locally, if an item 'for seking for lyme at Blickling' implies a successful search. However, there was a more distant source of lime, costing 3s 8d per load. Sand, too, was local, for its carriage cost a few pence per load. Baskets and lime sieves were purchased in Norwich.

Timber was the other basic construction material. Firs (ie laths) could be locally supplied in their thousands. Alders for scaffold poles were available not far away at Cawston. But suitable local timber trees for floor joists, for binders in the brick walls and for the roof trusses, soon ran out. At the outset trees were viewed 'in ye parke & wood & other grounds' and by early May 1619 308 trees had been felled. The following year it was a different story: the sources of timber were Morley, presumably Swanton Morley, ten miles away to the south-west, and Langley, the estate of a Hobart relative, twice as far away beyond Norwich.

The dressed stone, an excellent oolitic limestone, presumably from the Ketton quarries in North-amptonshire, would have been shipped down the River Welland to King's Lynn and so round the coast to Cley. Paving stone from Purbeck in Dorset came in by sea to Yarmouth and so up river to Coltishall. Other materials were acquired from the best sources all over the country: lead from Derbyshire, supplied by Thomas Cryre of Hassop and Sir George Manners; iron from John Midleton of Horsham in Sussex; and Newcastle glass from Sir Robert Mansell.

Changes to the original specifications, recorded in a 'note' dated 29 November 1619, make it possible to point to a number of improvements to the design which Lyminge incorporated while work was in progress. These changes, which increased the contract price, are of particular interest because they illuminate Lyminge's approach to architectural design. A major feature under discussion when the note was drafted was the wall fronting the moat before the entrance façade of the house. Lyminge pleaded against the proposed battlemented brick wall, which in his opinion 'will be very lumpish and will take away the prospect of the lower part of the house in the view of the court'. Instead he proposed 'open worke of stone', 3ft 6in high, to match the pierced stonework of the bridge, which had been cut at the quarry but was being held at the waterside until this decision had been resolved. In the end Lyminge got his way: his pierced balustrade, 'the Open Worke before the moat on the front', is costed at £47 in the note of the mason's work dated December 1620. Unfortunately this balustrade lasted for less than a century.

Hobart bulls above the entrance gateway flank escutcheons carved with the arms of Sir Henry Hobart and his wife, Dorothy Bell

The pierced work of the entrance bridge is all that survives now to show what it was like. Its ornamental arrow loops are the first evidence of the spurious air of military valour imparted to this lawyer's house.

The point at which a typical Elizabethan or Jacobean house made a display of the classical orders was at the entrance. A 'tower of the orders', with columns superimposed in three or even four tiers, constituted the most magniloquent piece of show possible at that period. Hatfield has a splendid example of such a tower. At Blickling the display is considerably more restrained: Doric columns, flanking two escutcheons of the family's arms. A final touch to the whole composition is given by the two little statues of Justice and Prudence, suitable for a lawyer, placed on the crest of the central window bay – they came cheap at £1 each.

Lyminge made two other changes to the design of the exterior of the house, both so subtle that one would hardly notice them if they were not documented, but both giving a little extra definition to the design. One concerned the tops of the turrets. Below the lead-covered turret-cap runs a full entablature, its cornice constructed of timber, the frieze and architrave of stone. The stone parts were not at first intended, and the weaker effect this would have had is demonstrated by the turrets at Hatfield, which have nothing but a cornice to crown the brickwork. The other improvement must also have been made to avoid another slightly disappointing effect at Hatfield. There, only the largest windows – those of six lights – had a thickened central mullion to subdivide them. At Blickling Lyminge decided that four-light windows should also be subdivided in this way.

Internally, the house was decorated with great richness and ostentation. On passing through the screens passage into the hall, the visitor was greeted by plaster figures set in niches high up in the walls of the Nine Worthies. They consisted of three pagan figures (Hector, Alexander and Julius Caesar), three Jewish (Joshua, David and Judas Maccabeus), and three Christian (Charlemagne, Arthur and Godfrey of Boulogne), who had established themselves in north European culture as epitomes of valour and virtue. The series was completed in 1627 when James Avis, plasterer, was paid £5 for the figure of Hector. They were in a sorry state by the middle of the 18th century, when Lord Buckinghamshire described them shortly before their removal (p. 49).

The Worthies were warriors and leaders of men. The military theme continued in the great staircase, which rose in a square well in three flights, its handrail carried on balusters linked at their feet by arcading. Every flight was marked by a strong, high newel post crowned by a figure, five of them in all. Against the walls were seven half posts, with two L-shaped ones in the angles. Most of these pieces survive in the present, much enlarged staircase, so

(Left) One of the Jacobean figures on the Great Staircase
(Right) A richly carved doorcase from the Jacobean staircase (now on the Staircase Gallery)

that their original arrangement can be envisaged. At the bottom stood a post, carved on its front face with musical instruments and a woman bearing a lute, and on the face towards the stairwell with what may be emblems of night: a bat, torches, a lantern on a hanging brazier. On top stood the striding figure of a bearded man wearing a mail collar and slashed breeches, holding a long two-handed sword. The free-standing post which may have stood on the first half-landing is carved with a trophy of armour, but the figure on it, in 16th-century costume, is not military, but looks rather more like a steward.

The conception of the staircase and many details of its carving relate it so closely to the Hatfield staircase that Lyminge must have been responsible for both, probably with the assistance of a specialist carver. At Hatfield the carver's name was John Bucke; his name does not occur in any of the accounts at Blickling, but then they fall silent between 1622 and May 1627, the period in which the staircase must have been constructed. All we do know is that in September 1623 Lyminge was in London, and one day went out with Lady Hobart to Hatfield.

Lyminge certainly made internal features at Blickling. The openwork pendant in the centre of the staircase ceiling, of timber plastered over, was his, and so was the magnificent columned chimneypiece in the great chamber (now the South Drawing Room). Neither of these required the services of a carver. The chimneypiece in the parlour immediately below (now the Dining Room) is scarcely less magnificent; with term figures instead of columns, it certainly needed a carver to execute the human elements. And here there is a detail which recurs on the staircase – the strings of discs which wreathe the torsos on the one and the newel-vases of the other.

Other stylistic connections lead a different way. Many of the staircase vases were carved with mask heads like those executed in stone in the courtyard doorways. These link timber-carving with stone-carving, a connection reinforced by the family likeness between the wreathed terms on the parlour chimneypiece and the wreathed terms which adorn the splendid stone doorcases, now on the Staircase

Gallery, but originally set at the head of the great stairs giving access to the great chamber and Long Gallery. These relationships suggest that the interior decoration was conceived as a whole, which in the circumstances of Jacobean design may mean no more than one person, presumably Lyminge, selecting appropriate engravings from which the craftsmen would work.

The most spectacular room in the house was the Long Gallery. The original full-height chimney-piece was removed in the mid-18th century; it was probably for this that Rowland Buckett (who had worked with Lyminge at Hatfield) gilded three pillars at a cost of £2 0s 4d in April 1624. But the glory of the room is the plaster ceiling, a dense and intricate pattern of bands enclosing heraldic and emblematic panels, the whole ceiling supported on a deep bracketed entablature. This is the first of the four ceilings by Edward Stanyon under his contract dated 11 August 1620. By 10 December it was finished, at a cost of £95 19s. These ceilings Stanyon was to execute 'according to such plottes & workemanship as now are or hereafter shall be drawne by Mr. Robert Lyming his Lordshipps Surveyor of the said workes'. However, before the signing of the contract the work 'drawne' was altered to 'directed'. So what 'direction' did Lyminge give to Stanyon? In artistic terms perhaps not much. The ceiling's basic design, the broad ribs decorated with foliage trails, and strapwork motifs in every spare space, has close parallels in other houses, for example Boston Manor, Middlesex (1623), and Langleys, Essex (c.1620). They could very well all be by Stanyon.

The emblematic subjects, on the other hand, are more likely to be the choice of Sir Henry Hobart, whose mantled shield of arms and motto occur in alternate panels running down the centre of the ceiling. The emblems come from *Minerva Britanna* (1612), by Henry Peacham, who may have been personally known to Sir Henry and other Hobarts. For he spent the years 1613–14 in Norwich as tutor to the sons of the Earl of Arundel. Of the 26 emblems in the gallery ceiling, all but the panels of the Senses derive from Peacham, who explained that their true use was 'to feede at once both the minde, and eie, by expressing mistically and doubt-

'Beauty is only skin deep': a plasterwork panel by Edward Stanyon on the ceiling of the Long Gallery

fully, our disposition, either to Love, Hatred, Clemencie, Iustice, Pietie, our Victories, Misfortunes, Griefes and the like: which perhaps could not have been openly, but to our praeiudice revealed'. Peacham includes explanatory verses under each emblem, which convey their meanings – mostly didactic or otherwise improving. Those chosen for Blickling express, among other things, womanly beauty and the power of love, kingly majesty and kingly cares, divine wisdom and pity, the need to trust God and to avoid hypocrites.

Off the Long Gallery, in the turret closet, Stanyon executed a strapwork ceiling featuring the Hobart bull in the centre. At the lower rate of 4s 6d per square yard it was set down in December 1620 as having cost £3 7s 6d. After that Stanyon must have moved on to the great chamber ceiling, which closely resembles the gallery's, with broad enriched bands and fanciful pendants, with low-relief strapwork patterns in the fields made by the bands. The withdrawing chamber was subdivided in the 18th century, so nothing of its 5s 6d ceiling or of its other decoration survives. The bedchamber beyond, and its turret closet, have plasterwork ceilings of a simpler design, more like the 4s 6d work of the gallery closet. So the plasterwork established a sort of hierarchy through the rooms of the principal suite. Doubtless their furnishings reinforced such distinctions, but unfortunately the earliest surviving inventory dates from 1698. All we know is that in 1627 Lyminge provided for the great chamber a table (p. 13) and rails 'above and below' for wall-hangings, presumably tapestries. The silk-covered furniture, chairs and stools, which John Baldwin, upholsterer of Norwich, was making in 1627, was intended for the 'dining chamber', ie for this room. This, too, would have been the place for Sir John to display on special occasions the rich plate bequeathed him by his father, in particular 'the greatest and most massie guilt plate' bequeathed 'for my eldest sonne, that is for my house'.

Nothing else is known for certain about how the state rooms at Blickling were furnished, but various purchases made in London when the house was nearing completion may have been intended for them. In October 1621 twelve pictures of sibyls were acquired for £9 12s. Early in 1622 Christopher Jenaway, upholsterer, supplied two suites of gilt leather hangings for £49 13s, and three large pieces of tapestry hangings at a cost of £21 13s 4d. Two years later Godfrey Holmes, another upholsterer, supplied five more pieces of tapestry for £20 7s and in December 1624 Matthew Bonny, a third member of the trade, sold to Hobart for £6 13s an old piece of tapestry hanging 'of the story of Hanyball Scipio'. The most valuable of these acquisitions was also second-hand: eight tapestries depicting the story of Abraham valued at £78 and acquired by Sir Henry in July 1624.

A further especially sumptuous set of furniture

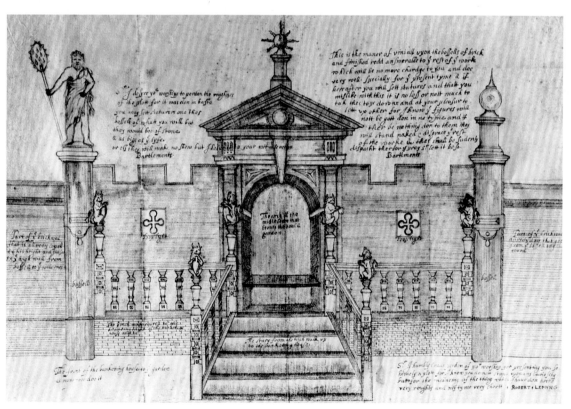

Robert Lyminge's only surviving design for Blickling: for a 'banketting house', or covered garden seat, which no longer survives

reached Blickling in due course. This was the embroidered scarlet bed, which, with its silk curtains, gold cups and the gilding of stools and chairs to match, cost at least £189 10s, mostly paid to Christopher Jenaway. This was a lying-in bed for John Hobart's second wife, Frances, the wealthy daughter of the Earl of Bridgewater, whom he married in 1621. In early December 1623 she was delivered of a son and heir, christened Henry after his grandfather, who threw a magnificent christening feast in celebration. Two months later the child was dead; so it must have been with a pang that Sir Henry paid Mr Greenway the 'comfittmaker' the colossal sum of £88 in August 1624. On the other hand another delayed bill, of £3 9s paid in April 1624 'for fringe &c for chayres and stooles suitable to the scarlet imbrothered bed against my Lady ffrances lyeing in', had to be seen as an investment for the future.

On the ground floor of the east range were other important rooms. The principal family living-room was the parlour. The parlour ceiling was one of the four for which Stanyon contracted at the top rate, so it is sad that the ceiling has not survived. However, the room's high status is indicated by the massive chimneypiece and overmantel bearing Sir Henry's arms and his motto in letters of especial boldness. Nothing else remains of the original arrangement of the ground floor of the east range. North of the great staircase lay the chapel, with its closet (the family pew), which was framed by six carved timber arches 'to looke out of the closet through the Chapple'. A pilastered doorcase and some steps led down into the chapel, where the servants would have had their seats. In 1627 Thomas Hamline of Norwich made and installed an organ, and Lyminge made some 'garnishing' for the top of it. In the same year chairs and stools covered with green cloth were also made for the chapel. Eventually, in January 1629, the Bishop of Norwich came and consecrated it.

Sir Henry Hobart seems to have visited his great house only once, in August 1624, and did not live to see it completed. He died in December 1625, leaving to his son the manor of Oulton to pay for the remaining building work and decoration. The bells of all the Norwich churches rang out to mark the passing of the great lawyer who, according to a contemporary, had possessed 'an excellent eloquence, the éclat of ancestry, the acutest abilities, the most engaging sweetness associated with a singular gravity'.

Sir John Hobart soon established a very different pattern of living from his father's. Sir Henry had spent most of his time in London, remaining active in the practice of the law, even going on circuit each spring, until his death, and his widow was established in the Highgate house. Sir John's life centred on the country. The account book of his personal expenses, kept by one of his stewards, Thomas Fowler, from 21 April 1627 to 25 March 1631, demonstrates it in surprising detail. This is the period when he and his family must have settled down into the new routine of life at Blickling. Almost ten months of each year, from early July until late April, were spent at Blickling, the remaining two months in London, with a period at midsummer for leisurely travel into the country visiting friends. Regular visitors in 1628 included Lord St John, Sir Miles Hobart of Intwood, and Sir Robert Bell, of the dowager Lady Hobart's family. Their presence is betrayed when Sir John Hobart loses to them at play, cards or dice, and his steward has to record his losses (ranging from 5s to £1). Play invariably took place in the parlour.

Lady Hobart had her own allowance, of £50 per quarter, but Sir John still had to pay for expensive clothes for Frances and Dorothy, his two daughters by his first wife. Not surprisingly, the buying of luxury items is recorded during the months when the family were in London, the 'great looking glasses' seen on approval on 30 May 1627 and bought for £3 the following day, and the two pictures delivered in June 1628 from the 'King's picture drawer' of a 'kitchenpiece' and a 'gally pott of Orrangeflowers'.

Sir John died in 1647, leaving only daughters. The estate was inherited by the youngest of these, Philippa, who had married her first cousin, John, son of Sir Miles Hobart of Intwood. This John also inherited the baronetcy, an unorthodox arrangement, emphasising the family's dynastic preoccupations in the early 17th century – preoccupations which were embodied in the building of Blickling.

GEORGIAN BLICKLING

Within two generations of its founding, the Lord Chief Justice's monument to the Hobart dynasty had entered a period of decline. John Hobart, 3rd Baronet, who succeeded in 1647, spent much of his life engaged in bitter and expensive political contests with his Tory opponent, Sir Robert Paston of Oxnead. Hobart, who had sat in Cromwell's short-lived Upper House, was 'the idol of the dissenting and "fanatique" elements in the county'. The Restoration proved only a temporary check on his career, and in 1671 a reconciliation was achieved when Charles II visited Blickling to be 'most noblie and plentifully treated in the great dining-room' (the present South Drawing Room). The King conferred a knighthood on Hobart's eldest son before departing for Oxnead where he was relieved to find himself 'safe in the House of His Friend'. Hobart returned to Parliament the

next year and after another decade of mutually exhausting political conflict both he and Paston expired in 1683. Hobart left his 26-year-old heir, Sir Henry, desperately in debt and Blickling mortgaged to John White, a London merchant, with its estate reduced to a quarter of the acreage of 1625.

John Pollexfen, another merchant to whom the mortgage of Blickling was assigned in the year of Sir John's death, was evidently used to dealing with the problems of impoverished baronets and suggested that if Sir Henry would find a lady who had between six and seven thousand a year acceptable, 'he would recommend such a one'. In the following year Hobart duly married Elizabeth, co-heir to Sir Joseph Maynard. A dowry of £10,000 released Blickling from its mortgage and allowed a momentary respite from financial problems.

The steward's account books for the following two decades depict a community of local people employed by the Hobarts about the house and estate. Widow Kytchen was paid quarterly 'for looking to the Rooms and Furniture' in the hall, while John Canseller waged war against rats; William Trappit the gardener invoiced for tools and watering pots, and directed the labours of the women and children who weeded the beds and walks; Thomas Knowles the glazier was paid annually for keeping Blickling's many windows in good repair; we hear of the bricklayers Joseph Balls and Robert Yaxley and, busiest of all, Thomas Burrows of Aylsham, the carpenter. Burrows is everywhere, moving timber barns, felling trees, building farmhouses and bridges, erecting palisades and, in the summer of 1695, making changes to the house which included the repair and modification of the east wing and moving the entrance of the Great Hall (p. 8). Even so, for Blickling the late 17th century is architecturally a conspicuously quiet period. Only a panelled parlour (now the Serving Room) survives from these years.

The 4th Baronet was a politician rather than a builder. His heavy expenditure on political campaigns would, in fact, ultimately have brought Blickling to its knees but for the events which followed the election of 1698. Incensed by rumours that his decisive defeat had been brought about by allegations of discreditable conduct at the Battle of

Sir Henry Hobart, 4th Bt, who was killed in a duel with a political opponent in 1698; attributed to William Wissing (Great Staircase)

the Boyne, where he had been an equerry to William III, Hobart accused his Tory neighbour Oliver Le Neve of Great Witchingham of circulating the stories and demanded satisfaction. They met in a futile contest on Cawston Heath in August 1698 where, contrary to expectation, the inexperienced and left-handed Le Neve managed to run his formidable opponent through. Hobart returned to Blickling to die the following day and Le Neve fled the country. A simple, early 18th-century monument at Cawston bearing the cryptic inscription 'HH' commemorates this catastrophe.

The estate was put in chancery for its five-year-old heir, Sir John, and the family relinquished its position in Norfolk politics. A quiet period of slow but continuous recovery followed. Some of Blickling's most important heirlooms had been sold to trustees, and in 1703 thirteen pictures were bought back by the steward, John Brewster. They included the Mytens portrait of Lord Chief Justice Hobart and the ancient double portrait of the founder of the family, Sir James Hobart with his wife.

In 1713, having completed his education at Clare Hall, Cambridge, Sir John Hobart set off to travel on the Continent; bills record sojourns at Lyons, Montpellier, Marseilles and Paris. He returned towards the end of the following year and in 1717 married Judith Britiffe, daughter of the Recorder of Norwich. For the second time in its history Blickling was put back on its feet by a large dowry, this time of £15,000.

The Hobarts, staunch supporters of the Parliamentary faction from Civil War days, had been running with the political tide since the Revolution of 1688, and by the beginning of the 18th century the Whigs, as they were now called, had established their pre-eminence. Sir John was elected MP for St Ives, Cornwall, in 1715 and again from 1722 to 1727; he was MP for Norfolk in 1727–8. Meanwhile his witty and attractive elder sister Henrietta, who had made an unhappy marriage to the future Earl of Suffolk, Charles Howard, had found favour at the Hanoverian court. She became the mistress of the Prince of Wales, and through her influence Hobart was made a Knight of the Bath in 1725, Treasurer of the Chamber in 1727, and Baron Hobart of Blickling in 1728.

Lord Hobart's contributions to the furnishing and adornment of Blickling announced his place in the Whig hierarchy. His sister Henrietta's charming portrait in masquerade dress is one of a great series culminating in the equestrian portrait of George II, which hung originally in the Long Gallery. William Aikman painted Hobart's friends, relatives and political allies in London in 1729. Minor Norfolk gentry like Edmund Prideaux and William Morden (later Harbord) of Gunton Hall are depicted as well as Whig grandees like Sir Robert Walpole, Thomas Coke and Lord Townshend. The rich Kent frames were very much in the Whig taste, and the windows of the gallery commanded a prospect of Hobart's new temple (first mentioned by a visitor in 1738), identical in its proportions and details to

John, 1st Earl of Buckinghamshire (1693–1756); by John Heins (Norwich Civic Portrait Collection)

William Kent's Holkham temple of 1729. Perhaps Kent himself was involved, or his executant architect at Holkham, Matthew Brettingham, who was later to undertake minor alterations at Blickling. However, at least one important undocumented change had been made to the house before 1725. Prideaux's drawing of the east front clearly shows the large doorway in the base of the north-east turret. This proves to have been the door which originally communicated between Lord Chief Justice Hobart's stair hall and the garden, and it may be that this opening, originally off-centre in the east façade, was moved because it offended the symmetry of the early 18th-century garden layout.

Hobart became Lord Lieutenant of Norfolk in 1739 and seven years later, having served on the Privy Council, was created Earl of Buckinghamshire. In spite of the high offices of state which he and his successor occupied, their resources left them no leeway to buy the choice works of art which were to fill other Norfolk houses at this time. But the library that came to Hobart from his distant cousin, Sir Richard Ellys of Nocton, probably on the remarriage of his widow in 1745, was one of the greatest collections of its kind. The Long Gallery was the only room at Blickling large enough to hold 10,000 books, so the full-length portraits were dispersed to other parts of the house. A group of craftsmen set to work making bookcases and decorations; Joseph Pickford made an expensive marble fireplace copied from one at Coleshill in Berkshire; Thomas Ivory appeared for the first time, probably employed as a carpenter at this early stage in his career; Scheemakers provided a bust of Sir Richard Ellys; Francis Hayman painted a series of overdoors; and John Cheere was paid for 28 busts, 20 vases and 3 statues, presumably all of plaster.

But the library was the only really significant addition made by the 1st Earl, and the description of the house in the valuation taken at his death in 1756 is dismissive: 'The house is very large, all the Rooms except those in the South Front are only common useful rooms with indifferent floors, wainscot and Common Marble Chimney Pieces the foundations begin to decay and it will be a continual expense to keep it in repair. The House is of something more Value than Materials.'

Henrietta Howard, Countess of Suffolk (c.1681–1767): 'of a just height, well made, extremely fair, with the finest light brown hair', according to Horace Walpole. She advised her nephew, the 2nd Earl of Buckinghamshire, on the remodelling of Blickling; attributed to Thomas Gibson, c.1720 (South Drawing Room)

In some ways Blickling was a daunting prospect at this period; the gradually crumbling Tudor ranges to the north and west, with their warren of wainscotted rooms, were an obvious drawback, and there were few landowners who would have warmed to the inconvenient and old-fashioned Jacobean work. It was Blickling's good fortune, therefore, that the new Lord Buckinghamshire was in tune with the most advanced architectural taste of the day, which in its enthusiasm for Gothick gladly joined turreted palaces of James I's reign with the medieval past.

John Hobart, 2nd Earl of Buckinghamshire (1723–93), having lost his mother at the age of four, spent a good deal of his childhood at Marble Hill House, Twickenham, in the care of his aunt, Henrietta Howard. One of the most perfect of Palladian villas, Marble Hill was the gift of the Prince of Wales to his mistress. Henrietta attracted the interest of some of the brightest stars of the early 18th-century court. Dilettanti like the earls of Pembroke and Burlington were often to be found at Marble Hill, as were the writers John Gay, Jonathan Swift and John Arbuthnot. Her neighbour Alexander Pope was a particular friend. He helped to lay out her garden and made her the subject of four laudatory verses *On a Certain Lady at Court*. Horace Walpole described the striking looks which she preserved into late age, 'of a just height, well made, extremely fair, with the finest light brown hair'. She shared his enthusiasm for amusing antiquities to the extent that in 1757 she asked one of his 'Committee of Taste', Dr Richard Bentley, to build her a steepled Gothick farm to which she gave the spurious dedication of 'St Hubert's Priory'.

The 2nd Earl's earliest alterations at Blickling were probably made in the early 1760s, when the Jacobean withdrawing chamber was divided into the Chinese Bedroom and its Dressing Room, both noticeably more rococo in character than the later alterations planned in 1765 after his diplomatic mission to Russia.

In August 1762 he was posted to St Petersburg as Ambassador at the Court of Catherine the Great. Horace Walpole's unkind characterisation of the young Buckinghamshire as 'the clearcake; fat, fair, sweet and seen through in a moment' describes adolescent qualities that developed in maturity into the good looks and amiable manners which it was hoped would please the Russian Empress. He attributed his failure to conclude the alliance between England and Russia in 1764 to the Treasury's meanness, but socially he was a success. His letters to Lady Suffolk from St Petersburg describe the Russian Court and its unfamiliar customs, the beauty of the Empress and her feats as a horsewoman. Buckinghamshire was particularly intrigued by the elaborate ceremonial of Court weddings and the contrasting informality of the

John, 2nd Earl of Buckinghamshire (1723–93), in his robes as Lord Lieutenant of Ireland; by Thomas Gainsborough, 1784 (Peter the Great Room)

balls, where all ranks and ages danced polonaises together, from 13-year-old maids of honour to octogenarian generals. Such entertainments were welcome diversions for an ambassador whose official duties were by no means onerous.

In the autumn of 1764 Buckinghamshire returned to England and the following year embarked on a programme of repair and modernisation which was to occupy many happy years at Blickling. His architects were Thomas Ivory and his son William. The drawings of the 2nd Earl's alterations were made in 1765 and somewhat amended and supplemented in 1767. But there are earlier designs which could have been made around 1760, and it is known that Buckinghamshire

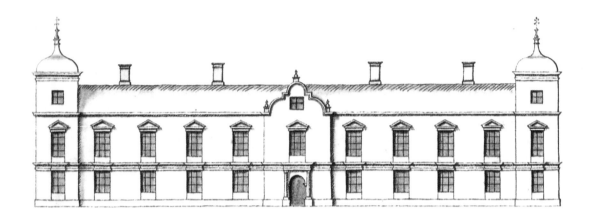

An early proposal of c.1760 for remodelling the west front, which reflects the 2nd Earl's concern to retain the Jacobean character of the house

consulted Matthew Brettingham over alterations at Blickling before 1762. These early plans show the remodelling of the west front with a central, neo-Jacobean gable and sash-windows throughout, with alternative schemes for the recasting of the north front. In all cases the elevations show the towers reduced in height to something more like the scheme followed by many Palladian tower-houses of the 18th century – Holkham (1732) and Kimberley (1763) are two local examples – whereas the later designs retained them at full height. The importance of these early drawings is that they indicate an attempt to reflect the Jacobean character of the house; they are forerunners of the 2nd Earl's final scheme which was in itself one of the earliest instances of Jacobean revival.

The 2nd Earl's work was planned in close consultation with his aunt. 'Nothing is more amusing', he wrote to her in November 1765, 'than to see numbers of workmen within and without doors: it is not exactly the same thing to pay their bills ... Lady Buckinghamshire [Mary Anne Drury, his first wife] and Lady Dorothy [his sister] have entered into a conspiracy against the old chimney piece in the eating-room. Their little intrigues can never shake my settled purpose, but they tease me and your authority is necessary to silence them.'

William Ivory's 1765 design for the north front

It is obvious that these words were not written with an entirely straight face, like another letter about the same room written later in that month: 'Gothic it was, and more Gothic it will be, in spite of all the remonstrances of modern improvers and lovers of Grecian architecture. The ceiling is to be painted with the loves of Cupid and Psyche. Cupid is to hover exactly over the centre of the table, to indicate to the maître d'hôtel the exact position of the venison pasty.'

Buckinghamshire also let Lady Suffolk have news of the radical changes that were proposed for the Great Hall in this year:

I have determined what is to be done with the Hall which you ought to approve, and indeed must approve. Some tributary sorrow should be paid to the nine worthies; but Hector has lost his spear and his nose, David his harp, Godfrey of Boulogne his ears, Alexander the Great his highest shoulder, and part of Joshua's belly is fallen in. As the ceiling is to be raised eight of them must have gone, and Hector is at all events determined to leave his niche.

He goes on to name the eight 'worthies' of his own time, politicians whose 'figures are not as yet essentially mutilated', as possible replacements and suggests that 'as Anne Boleyn was born at Blickling, it will not be improper to purchase her father [sic] Henry the Eighth's figure (which by order is no longer to be exhibited at the Tower) who will fill with credit the space occupied by the falling Hector'.

This valuable description of the Jacobean decoration in the Great Hall also shows that even though the 'eight worthies' project was not a serious one, the reliefs in niches of Queen Elizabeth and Anne Boleyn originated in the ancient scheme. In 1767 they were placed above the landings of a great double-flight staircase to which the Great Hall was now given over. It incorporated nearly all the timbers of the old Jacobean staircase, removed from the original site in the east front. The Ivorys' efforts to match the old timbers in softwood were more than adequate and in places it is quite difficult to distinguish their work from that of the Jacobean craftsmen. Some of their newel figures, however, are distinctly and deliberately modern. To make a decent approach to the stair foot and allow room for a gallery to communicate between the east and west ranges, the front wall of the Great Hall was demolished and rebuilt so that it stood proud of the flanking turrets in the Stone Court.

The removal of the Jacobean staircase allowed the creation of a comfortable suite of rooms on the ground floor of the east range. A floor was introduced in the stairwell to create a 'Drinking Room' (the present Lower Ante-Room) and on the first floor a tapestried ante-chamber to the Long Gallery and drawing-room. The ground-floor rooms to the north were Lady Buckinghamshire's dressing-room and bedchamber (taking in the present Brown Room) and the 'Tool Closet' (carpentry was evidently a hobby of his Lordship's and the inventory of 1793 reverentially records the single product

The Great Hall as remodelled with a double-flight staircase in 1767; watercolour by J.C. Buckler, 1829 (Great Hall)

of his pleasurable labours, 'My Lord's Paddle'). Further along the corridor was the 'Physic closet', which in 1793 contained an apparatus 'for Electrifying'; the use of mild shocks from static electricity was one of the health fads of the late 18th century. At the end was Lord Buckinghamshire's study with windows facing east and north. In 1773 a staircase was installed in the adjacent turret to connect the study with the Library in the Long Gallery above.

As work proceeded on the great staircase, the medieval west range was being refronted and extensively remodelled. William Ivory's design for this elevation was one of the least successful aspects of Lord Buckinghamshire's work. It had a completely straight parapet and, as its only concession to the Jacobean ranges, there were mullioned windows. It must have been this part of the building that prompted Silas Neville, who saw Blickling in 1782, to remark that 'The new part is very inferior and looks more like an hospital than a nobleman's seat'. Lady Suffolk's death in 1767 was rapidly followed by that of the young Lady Buckinghamshire in 1769, and an inscription in the centre of the new west front records that her jewels were bequeathed to pay for its completion.

In 1770 Buckinghamshire married his second wife, Caroline, daughter of Sir William Conolly of Stratton Hall, Staffordshire. In 1777 he became Lord Lieutenant of Ireland. It was an uncomfortable appointment, compromised by his relationship to the Conolly family – his brother-in-law, Thomas Conolly of Castletown, was one of the most vocal members of the Irish Parliament – and, despite the passage of several useful reforms, it was, by common consent, a failure. With relief he was able to return to England late in 1780, describing himself as 'a man whose mind has been ulcerated with a variety of embarrassments for thirty weary months'. In his absence, Thomas and William Ivory had been pushing ahead with the completion of the north front, whose overall design, set out in William Ivory's drawing of 1765, was finalised in 1768, when it was decided to have a flat lead roof, a stone balustrade and pedimented windows. It is an outstanding example of 'keeping in keeping' and even the texture and bond of the brickwork is virtually indistinguishable from the Jacobean work.

The ground-floor rooms here were well advanced by the time that the west wing was being fitted out in 1773, and the principal apartment at this level was the Organ Chamber. Strongly antiquarian in character, its doors and ceiling were decorated with small swirls of Gothick tracery. The medieval angels from Caister Castle, bought from the sale of Oxnead in 1732, were incorporated into the fireplace (removed to the Brown Drawing Room in 1858).

By November 1778 John Ivory, the marble mason, was being paid 100 guineas for a Sienna marble fireplace for the 'great room', now known as the Peter the Great Room, occupying the three central bays of the first floor. The Peter the Great

Caroline Conolly, who married the 2nd Earl in 1770; by Thomas Gainsborough, 1784 (Peter the Great Room)

The Orangery was probably built by Samuel Wyatt in 1782

Room and its adjoining State Bedroom are the two most important 18th-century rooms at Blickling. They were conceived as a setting for the works of art which commemorated the high point of Buckinghamshire's career when he was Ambassador at St Petersburg: the spectacular tapestry of Peter the Great at the Battle of Poltawa, presented to him by Catherine the Great in 1764, as well as the two portraits of George III and Queen Charlotte, and the rich canopy of state which had accompanied his diplomatic mission.

In April 1779 Thomas Ivory was badly injured when his leg was crushed by a piece of timber and by late May his health was in 'a Dangerous and alarming state with strong symptoms of mortification'. Unable to stir from his bed, he would naturally have hoped that his son William would take over the work. But the country was now involved in a colonial war with France and, with the threat of invasion, militia companies were drilling all over England. Captain William Ivory, who could not be released from the manoeuvres of Sir John Wodehouse's militia at Coxheath camp, suggested that 'Mr Wyat' at London might undertake the carpenter's work at Blickling.

Samuel Wyatt was one of the leading exponents of 18th-century Neo-classicism and by May 1780 was already directing alterations at the Buckinghamshires' Bond Street house. The architecture of the State Bedroom at Blickling is so remarkably

self-assured that it is hard to believe that the Ivorys, who had obvious difficulty assimilating new Neo-classical ideas in the Peter the Great Room, were responsible for it. Samuel Wyatt must have designed this beautiful room, though the basic plan, which is exactly the same as Lady Suffolk's bedchamber at Marble Hill, is that of William Ivory, who early in 1779 submitted designs adapted 'in some measure to the stile of the House'. The decoration and furnishings here and in the Peter the Great Room were being completed in 1782.

It is possible to follow Lord Buckinghamshire's work at Blickling in such detail partly through correspondence with his conscientious but not always tactful agent, Robert Copeman. Despite Copeman's opposition, the 2nd Earl turned to Wyatt for the new Orangery, which strongly recalls his vine house at Holkham in its reserved use of Coade stone plaques and its marvellously delicate fanlights.

Having essentially completed the restoration of the house, Lord Buckinghamshire spent the last decade of his life in making adjustments. Water closets were installed, probably for the first time, in 1791, and small changes were made in the garden. Copeman's letter book of 1789–92 and the 2nd Earl's letters to his youngest daughter, Amelia, addressed as 'Dear Baby', reveal glimpses of a quiet life at Blickling.

In 1792, he secured Caroline's marriage with

Caroline, Lady Suffield (d.1850), who inherited Blickling in 1793; by Thomas Lawrence (private Scottish collection)

William Harbord, heir to his near neighbour, Lord Suffield of Gunton. The family came to stay that December, when Lord and Lady Suffield were pleased to be given a warm room above the kitchen in the west range. Lord Buckinghamshire was solicitous for his son-in-law's health. 'Mr Harbord's gout is so far better that he walked yesterday to the Greenhouse. Such an attack is very unpleasant circumstance so early in life, it indeed concerns me to think that neither he nor Caroline will ever enjoy vigorous health.'

Lord Buckinghamshire was himself a victim of this common 18th-century complaint, and, according to Horace Walpole, his death in 1793 was brought about by thrusting an inflamed foot into a bucket of icy water. On the 2nd Earl's death the title passed to his brother George, while Blickling went to his second daughter Caroline. His eldest daughter, Harriet, had incurred her father's displeasure by divorcing the Earl of Belmore in 1791; two years later she married the Earl of Ancram, who was later to become 6th

Marquess of Lothian. Caroline and her husband, who became Lord Suffield in 1810, were childless so that the succession passed to the Lothians on Lord Suffield's death in 1821. Lady Suffield, however, lived on at Blickling until 1850.

Surprisingly little is known about the long tenure of Lady Suffield. She and her husband invited the fashionable London architect Joseph Bonomi to design a striking pyramidal mausoleum for the 2nd Earl, and in the first quarter of the 19th century the austere rooms of the Georgian house were given some of the comforts of the Regency. But it was not until the late 1820s that Lady Suffield made her mark on the house. She was an enterprising gardener and had employed Humphry Repton and his eldest son John at Gunton. In the 1820s John Adey Repton also worked on the garden at Blickling and on some of the buildings of the estate. A prolific writer on antiquarian subjects, he made additions to the house that were more scholarly and correct than even the most literal Jacobean essays of the Ivorys. Repton submitted a design for the reconstruction of the central clock-tower in *c.*1828, which, with minor changes, was carried out. The linking arcades between the house and wings are also his, and there are drawings for neo-Jacobean furniture, some of which remained at Blickling until the 1930s. He also provided drawings for the ornamentation of the parish church.

Blickling twice escaped destruction by fire during the early part of the 19th century. The first was in 1808: people came from Aylsham to fight the blaze and gratuities were distributed in the town afterwards. The second broke out in April 1849, and was described by Lady Suffield's agent, Robert Parmeter, who wrote:

Mr. C. Marsham, who fortunately was staying in the House, informs me that but for the courage of his own servant, the under Butler & principal Footman of Lady Suffield and Mr Wells the Innkeeper … who exposed themselves to the fire and smoke of the Room almost to suffocation until the Flames were extinguished … it would have been impossible to save the house.

Lady Suffield died in the following year, aged 83, and was buried at Gunton. At last the Lothian family, for whom Blickling had been destined since 1821, could take full possession of the house.

BLICKLING UNDER THE LOTHIANS

William Schomberg Robert Kerr (pronounced 'Karr') was nine years old when he became 8th Marquess of Lothian, and eighteen when he inherited Blickling. On his father's side, his forebears were a Scottish border family whose titles included the barony of Jedburgh and the earldom of Ancram; his mother was a Talbot. At Oxford he moved mostly in Catholic and High Anglican circles, no doubt influenced by his mother's earlier conversion to Catholicism. At Oxford, too, he met the architect William Butterfield and the inventive and adventurous decorative painter and architect John Hungerford Pollen.

In 1854 Lord Lothian married his first cousin, Lady Constance Talbot. Among the couple's friends in London were more notable artists: G.F. Watts was to become the confidant of Lady

William, 8th Marquess of Lothian (1832–70), who commissioned J.H. Pollen to redecorate several of the principal rooms at Blickling; by G.F. Watts (private Scottish collection)

Lothian, and her husband's early diaries record musical evenings at the home of Val Prinsep.

During the early years of their marriage, the Lothians frequently travelled to France and Italy, and in 1854 they had spent many months in India, chiefly in the north and in Tibet. Early photographs of Blickling show how the rooms were furnished with their purchases. The family owned a large number of other houses, including Newbattle Abbey in Lothian, a huge and rambling mansion incorporating monastic remains, and the border castle of Ferniehurst. In the 1850s and '60s the couple were constantly on the move, staying at Scottish fishing lodges, with the Talbots at Ingestre, the Salisburys at Hatfield and at their own London house in Upper Grosvenor Street.

Before departing for his travels in Asia, Lothian made arrangements for a memorial window to Lady Suffield at Blickling church. It was the collaborative effort of Butterfield and John Hardman, whose stained glass – the first to recover the strength and purity of medieval painting – Lothian had admired in some of the newly built High Anglican churches in London. The Blickling window, a masterpiece of clear delineation and brilliant, jewel-like colour, was installed in the spring of 1856.

After their return to England in 1856, the renovation of Blickling became a major preoccupation for the Lothians. The division and enlargement of some of Lord Buckinghamshire's ground-floor rooms on the east front was the first job and by 4 December 1857 the house was 'in all the confusion and *desolation* of Bricklayers and carpenters', who were busy forming a new morning-room (the present Brown Drawing Room). The architect of this work was Benjamin Woodward, the designer of the Debating Hall at the Oxford Union built in 1857, where Pollen, Morris, Burne-Jones, Rossetti, Val Prinsep and others worked together on the spectacular but now much-faded mural decoration. In the following year Pollen had joined Woodward at Blickling, devising for the morning-room a wonderful beamed ceiling decorated with entwined birds and serpents painted on strips of canvas. This highly original decoration survives above a later suspended ceiling and is recorded in drawings and photographs.

Constance, Marchioness of Lothian (1836–1901),
who created the Parterre garden; by John Leslie, 1866
(Brown Drawing Room)

Just as remarkable in its way was the ceiling of Lady Lothian's sitting-room at the north end of the east front, in which Pollen painted broad bands of Celtic interlace over a sky of wheeling birds; it has long since been painted over. In the Long Gallery, however, much of his decoration remains. The work here coincided with the construction of the University Museum in Oxford where Woodward worked with Pollen and two gifted Irish sculptors, the brothers O'Shea. Lord Lothian, a generous contributor to the Museum Sculpture Fund, was able to involve this team at Blickling. By 1858 the books had been removed from the room and in the following year carpenters were recasting the 1st Earl's presses into the new powerful Gothic profile, and John O'Shea began to carve their uprights into naturalistic foliage, inspired no doubt by local trees and plants, just as specimens from Oxford's Botanical Gardens had been lovingly copied for the

Museum. A huge hooded marble chimneypiece arrived in 1860; Gothic in overall form, it was carved to Pollen's design with strange birds, Islamic patterns and, in the centre, two Hobart bulls carved in low relief and facing each other like the figures in the Lion Gate at Mycenae, beneath a tree hung with heraldry. The fireplace has gone but the extraordinary eclecticism of its decoration is recalled by the painted frieze around the upper walls of the gallery. Here Renaissance white vine interlace – inspired perhaps by the 15th-century Suetonius manuscript which is one of the greatest treasures of the Blickling library – coils round figures of art and literature before a strongly rendered Khelim backcloth. Curtains of woven strips, decorated with Pollen's designs, were made in Algeria. In February 1861 the Lothian's agent, Robert Parmeter, wrote to express his concern that the estate was running out of money and to advocate economies. The carving and some of Pollen's painted decoration was left unfinished, but the rest of the project was completed by 1863.

Lord Lothian had gradually instituted improvements to make Blickling a more comfortable house. The waterworks were reorganised in 1857, gas was introduced in the following year, and in 1862 Haden & Jones of Trowbridge had installed a 'warming apparatus' whose grills are still visible. The bedrooms of the west front had been redecorated and refurnished, each known by a letter of the word Lothian in imitation of the 18th-century Buckingham Row on the top floor. Now William Burn, the aged and highly respected country-house architect who had done so much to establish the neo-Jacobean style and who had worked at Newbattle in 1836, was called in to devise improvements to the domestic offices and other areas.

Burn's job was to plan a new range of offices in the west wing and provide servants' accommodation. The west wing was completely rebuilt, retaining only its Jacobean front wall, to accommodate a new kitchen, laundry, brew-house and game larders. Burn had hoped to build accommodation for servants in a structure that would have joined this wing to the house but Lord Lothian was emphatic that Blickling's appearance should not be spoilt by this addition, and the accommodation was squeezed into the lower floors of the west front.

But the 8th Marquess was not long to enjoy these improvements, and in 1870, at the age of 38, he finally succumbed to the disease which he is thought to have contracted in India and which had latterly confined him to a wheelchair. Eight years later, G.F. Watts carved for the church a stupendous effigy of veined alabaster, attended by life-sized angels. Lady Lothian's restoration of the church, undertaken in two phases, in 1872 and 1876, was also a memorial to her husband, and for the first time since perhaps the 17th century the tower was raised to a height that allowed the church to make its presence felt in a village that had hitherto been completely dominated by the house, a practical demonstration of the power of Victorian piety. The principal consolation of Lady Lothian's long widowhood, however, was the development of the gardens at Blickling (see p. 31).

From Lady Lothian's death in 1901, Blickling was let to tenants until 1932, when Philip Kerr, 11th Marquess of Lothian, decided to make the

J.H. Pollen's design for the Long Gallery chimneypiece, which was removed in the 1930s

house his principal English seat. Kerr, who had somewhat reluctantly inherited his title two years earlier, was a man of vision and ability who was to play a crucial part in the international diplomacy of the Second World War before his premature death in 1940. A convinced Liberal, he became private secretary to Lloyd George in 1916 and drafted the preface to the Treaty of Versailles in 1919. He resigned in 1921 to devote more time to journalism and travel in his capacity as Secretary of the Rhodes Trustees. In 1931, when he joined the all-party Cabinet of Ramsay MacDonald, he was made Chancellor of the Duchy of Lancaster and, a few months later, Under-Secretary of State for India. He resigned from the administration in 1932 when he found its politics incompatible with his strong belief in Free Trade. It was at this time that he turned his attention to Blickling, which he saw as a quiet place for writing and for gatherings of politicians and academics, especially the meetings of *The Round Table*, an influential quarterly journal devoted to Imperial and Commonwealth politics, of which he had been the founding editor in 1910.

Lothian was an idealist and something of an eccentric. His friends despaired of his untidy appearance, which was redeemed by boyish good looks and a lack of self-consciousness typified by his arrival at Westminster Abbey for the coronation of George VI in an Austin 7. Some of his earliest visits to Blickling were made on a much-loved motorcycle.

After years of letting, Lothian found the house gloomy and drab; its rooms cluttered with Victorian furniture whose arrangement had been muddled by successive tenants, in a state of unattractive decay. It took 33 workmen fourteen months to bring Blickling up to date. The Great Hall was painted white, its stained glass and many of the full-length portraits were removed and stored. Elsewhere in the house much of the powerful and idiosyncratic high Victorian decoration was painted out or otherwise concealed; Sheraton and Chippendale furniture was bought to replace the Victorian pieces. Lothian appears to have been influenced by Christopher Hussey's articles in *Country Life* in 1930, which criticised the fireplace in the Long Gallery and the elaborate Parterre of

Lady Lothian. With hindsight, the destruction of the fireplace was very regrettable, but the transformation of the Parterre and the simplification of the Victorian planting in the Temple Walk was an inspired piece of gardening (see p. 32).

Lord Lothian stayed at Blickling only for short periods, but this was the last time the Hall operated on a full scale, with an establishment of twelve resident domestic servants. On some weekends there were 36 fires for the housemaids to tend and on still autumn afternoons a pall of smoke would hang over the house. At Round Table 'moots' Lord Halifax, Sir Edward Grigg, Lionel Curtis and Lord and Lady Astor would congregate at an oak table in the South Drawing Room for meetings which often included foreign diplomats and men of affairs from Commonwealth countries.

Although he had no taste for shooting, Lothian allowed the Astors' sons to do so. On the occasions when their parents accompanied them, Nancy Astor would lower the blinds in order not to witness the carnage, and there was an atmosphere of restraint, but on other weekends the housemaids would have to clear up the debris of cut-flower fights and bath salt battles.

Lord Lothian's political reputation was somewhat tarnished by his association with the Cliveden set and their advocacy of Appeasement in the run up to the Second World War. Von Ribbentrop, Nazi Germany's ambassador at the Court of St James, stayed at Blickling in 1934 and left his arrogant signature in the visitors' book. But Lord Lothian was to play a leading part in defeating Hitler during the short period of his embassy at Washington in 1939–40. It was he who persuaded Churchill to write the historic letter to Roosevelt which for the first time gave the Americans an unequivocal statement of Britain's depleted military strength. At a daringly timed press conference in Washington, Lothian delivered a similar message to the American public, helping to create a political climate that allowed the President to give substantial assistance to the Allies. This was the culmination of months of travel and speeches by Lothian which, in stressing America's interest rather than the plight of the Allies, had helped to turn opinion across the United States. Tragically, this punishing schedule took its toll of Lothian's health. Some years earlier, under the influence of Nancy Astor, he had become a Christian Scientist. Now his beliefs would not allow him to submit to medical treatment.

Just before one of his last trips to Washington, Lothian, standing at the window gazing out over the lake at Blickling, remarked to Miss O'Sullivan, his secretary, 'Now that it has come to the point, I don't want to go; I may never see this again'. Whether these words were prompted by the general insecurity of the times or some sense of his own impending death, is uncertain, but he saw Blickling only once more, in October 1940, when in a brief and busy visit to England, he spent a day at the house which had since been requisitioned as the Officers' Mess for RAF Oulton. He ordered some of the soft furnishings which had been put away for safekeeping to be brought out to make the officers more comfortable. He returned to Washington in November 1940 and died of uremic poisoning on 12 December.

Philip, 11th Marquess of Lothian (1882–1940), who bequeathed Blickling to the National Trust; posthumous portrait by James Gunn (Dining Room)